SPITFIRE

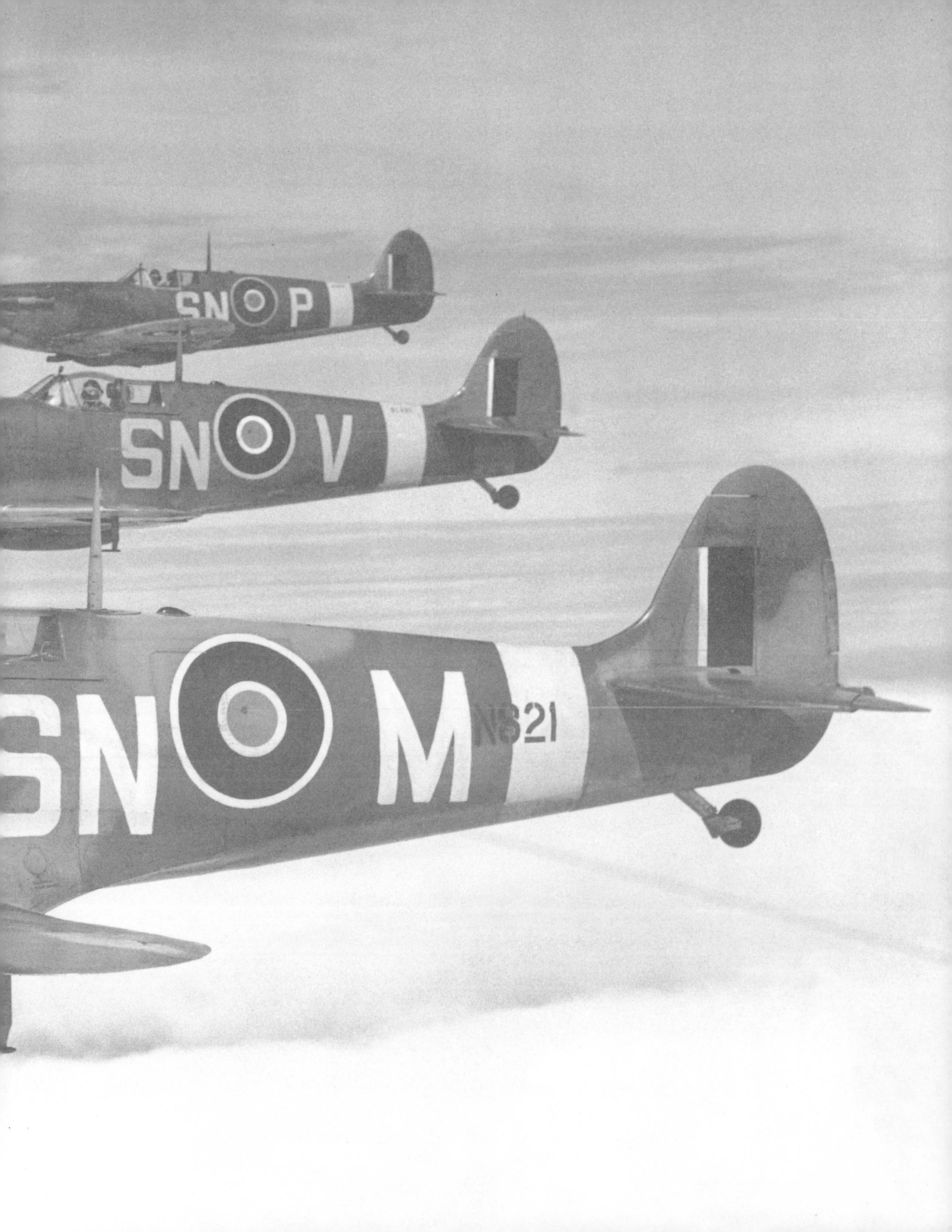
SN P
SN V
SN M
N3821

SPITFIRE

THE HISTORY OF BRITAIN'S MOST FAMOUS WORLD WAR II FIGHTER

ROBERT JACKSON

p

This is a Parragon Book
First published in 2003

Parragon
Queen Street House
4 Queen Street
Bath BA1 4HE, UK

Copyright © Parragon 2003

ISBN 0-75258-770-6

Editorial and design by
Amber Books Ltd
Bradley's Close
74–77 White Lion Street
London N1 9PF
www.amberbooks.co.uk

A copy of the CIP data for this book is available from the British Library.

Printed in China

CONTENTS

CHAPTER ONE

Ancestral Lines

The name 'Spitfire' has become a household word in the English language, not just by identification with a particularly beautiful fighter aircraft, but also as a symbol of defiance from the darkest days of World War II. Mention the word Spitfire to anyone, even all these years later, and it will be greeted with a smile of understanding.

Opposite: Royal Air Force personnel examining K5054, the Supermarine Spitfire prototype. The early two-bladed wooden propeller was soon replaced by a metal three-bladed one.

Below: Staff of the Supermarine Aviation Works, Southampton, with HRH the Prince of Wales in 1924. R.J. Mitchell, designer of the Spitfire, is third from the right, front row.

Mention the name Supermarine Baby, on the other hand, and it will probably be greeted with a blank look. The Baby was the first British fighter flying boat. Only one example was built, but the concept led to the development of two more designs, the Sea King and the Sea Lion; and all three aircraft were the first links in a chain of development that would lead directly to the Spitfire.

The Sea King, powered by a 119kW (160hp) Beardmore engine, attracted a lot of interest but no customers. The Sea Lion, with a 224kW (300hp) Hispano-Suiza powerplant, was entered in the 1919 Schneider Trophy contest and performed well, despite the fact that its hull got holed and the pilot lost himself in fog. In the 1922 contest, Supermarine entered the Sea Lion II, which was the original Sea Lion rebuilt as a racing flying boat and powered by a 336kW (450hp) Napier Lion engine. Piloted by Captain H.C. Biard, the Sea Lion II won the contest with comparative ease, completing the 370km (200nm) course in 1 hour 34 minutes and 54 seconds at an average speed of 234.4km/h (145.7mph) and beating three Italian entries.

Talented

The Sea Lion II was the brainchild of a talented young designer named Reginald Mitchell. Mitchell joined Supermarine in 1916 as assistant to Hubert Scott-Paine, chief engineer and designer (the company had been founded in 1912 by the pioneer

aviator Noel Pemberton-Billing, who had built his first flying boat in 1913, and was based at Woolston, on the Itchen river near Southampton). In 1920, Scott-Paine appointed Mitchell chief engineer and designer on projects that were mainly concerned with military flying boats.

The key to the whole task of producing a successful high-speed aircraft was the powerplant, and it was their technical skill in building high-performance aero-engines which enabled the

Above: Against the background of the setting sun, Supermarine S6 N248 is manoeuvred to her moorings. Her sister aircraft, N247, won the 1929 Schneider Trophy contest.

Americans and French to establish a commanding lead in the years immediately after World War I. In 1920-23 racing variants of the Nieuport-Delage 29 fighter, fitted with a 239kW (320hp) Hispano-Suiza engine, improved on the world absolute air speed record seven times, as well as capturing numerous trophies, while Curtiss CR-3 biplanes powered by 298kW (400hp) Curtiss D12 engines achieved first and second places in the Schneider Trophy contest.

These foreign successes prompted the leading British aero-engine manufacturers to re-examine their engine design philosophy. As a result Rolls-Royce produced the Kestrel, which represented a considerable advance over the Curtiss D12 and was selected to power the Hawker Hart light bomber and Hawker Fury fighter. The Kestrel in its ultimate form – the Kestrel V – later developed into the PV12, the prototype of the engine that was to play such an enormous part in World War II, the Rolls-Royce Merlin.

Destroyed

But in the early 1920s Rolls-Royce were not yet in a position to combine engine reliability with high performance, and in 1925 it was a 522kW (700hp) Napier Lion engine that powered Reginald Mitchell's entry for that year's Schneider Trophy contest, the Supermarine S4. Unfortunately, the aircraft crashed and was totally destroyed on the day before the race, Henry Biard narrowly escaping with his life. A 653kW (875hp) Napier Lion was also selected to power the Supermarine S5 in the 1926 contest, but the engine was not delivered in time for the aircraft to take part and the race was won by an Italian Macchi M.39. The S5 was ready in time for the 1927 contest, and won it with an average speed of 453.282 km/h (281.49mph), setting up a new 100km closed circuit world seaplane speed record into the bargain.

For the 1927 competition, held in Venice, the British entry was an all-RAF affair, a special unit known as the High Speed Flight having been formed for the occasion. There was no contest in 1928, but the High Speed Flight's development work continued at Felixstowe, and in February 1929 the Air Ministry once again decided to enter a team. This time, Rolls-Royce were asked to provide the engine for Mitchell's latest racing design, the Supermarine S6. To cut a few corners, as time was running short, Rolls-Royce decided to modify an existing engine, the 615kW (825hp) Buzzard (virtually a scaled-up Kestrel). The engine that emerged was the 'R' type, strengthened and fitted with a large double-sided centrifugal supercharger. These improvements increased the engine's power at sea level to a massive 1380kW (1850hp).

Technical challenges

While Rolls-Royce worked to overcome some fuel problems that had arisen during development of the 'R' type, Reginald Mitchell had been tailoring his S6 seaplane design to fit around the new engine. His estimate was that the aircraft would be capable of a speed in the order of 644km/h (400mph), and his figures included a level speed of 563km/h (350mph), a diving speed of 842km/h (523mph) and a rate of climb of 1525m (5000ft) per minute. In fact, these estimates were to reappear as the design characteristics for the Spitfire.

Despite a number of technical problems the Supermarine S6, flown by Flt Lt H.R.D. Waghorn, went on to win the 1929 Schneider Trophy contest at Spithead with a speed of 531.20km/h (330mph). On 12 September one of the other High Speed Flight pilots, Sqn Ldr A.H. Orlebar, flew the aircraft

to a new world seaplane speed record of 575.53km/h (357.7mph) over a 100km closed circuit. These were phenomenal speeds for their time, and should have encouraged the British Government to invest in further development of both aircraft and engine. But the Government announced that it was no longer prepared to subsidize RAF participation in the contest (which was now held over two years) on grounds of cost, and economic uncertainty.

The news was received with bitter disappointment by all concerned, because Britain had won two consecutive contests – if the British could win a third, they could keep the coveted trophy permanently. It was only thanks to the intervention of Lady Houston, a great patriot and philanthropist, who donated £100,000, that the

Above: **Supermarine S6B S1595 being pre-flight checked prior to its uncontested winning of the 1931 Schneider Trophy outright for Britain. The aircraft was powered by a Rolls-Royce 'R' engine.**

Below: **The Supermarine Type 224, K2890. Designed to meet the requirements of F7/30, it was not a success, one of the problems being the steam-cooled Rolls-Royce Goshawk engine.**

situation was rescued. Instead of taking up a new design, as time was now short, Mitchell set about modifying the two existing S6s by fitting them with enlarged floats and re-designating them S6As. He then built two new machines, based on the existing airframe but incorporating much more powerful Rolls-Royce 'R' engines developing 1753kW (2350hp). The new aircraft were designated S6B.

Suddenly, the British found themselves with no competitors. The Italians could not produce an aircraft in time, and the French entry had crashed during trials, killing the pilot. Nevertheless, the 'contest' went ahead, and on 13 September 1931 Flt Lt J.W. Boothman flew S6B S1595 over the seven laps of the 50km course at an average speed of 547.188km/h (340.08mph). That same afternoon, Flt Lt G.H. Stainforth set up a new world speed record of 609.89km/h (379.05mph) in the other S6B, S1596. Later, on 29 September, Stainforth pushed the world speed record up to 655.66km/h (407.5mph).

Peril

Both S6Bs are preserved today, one (S1595) in the Science Museum, London, and the other (S1596) at Southampton. They brought the Schneider Trophy back to Britain for all time, but more importantly, they and their progenitors made a contribution to the development of high-speed aerodynamics and high-powered engines that, within a decade, would help the nation to survive her hour of greatest peril.

In the autumn of 1930 the Air Ministry issued specification F7/30, which called for a single-seat monoplane day and night fighter with a speed of at least 314km/h (195mph), exceptional manoeuvrability, long endurance, a low landing speed, high initial rate of climb and excellent all-round view. It was to be

armed with four 7.7mm (0.303in) Vickers guns, and R/T equipment was to be fitted. F7/30 was the most important specification issued so far, because it attempted to sweep aside the inadequacies of the contemporary generation of biplane fighters. Supermarine, Westland, Blackburn, Bristol and Gloster all tendered designs to meet it.

The aircraft developed by Supermarine (named the Type 224) was an all-metal monoplane with a thick inverted gull wing and short cantilever undercarriage, the aerodynamic design having been subjected to much wind tunnel testing. It was powered by a Rolls-Royce Goshawk engine. The F7/30 was Mitchell's first attempt to apply the aerodynamic knowledge derived from the Supermarine Schneider racers to a land-based fighter design, and he was far from happy with the result. Nevertheless, the aircraft was built, and on 19 February 1934 it was flown by Supermarine test pilot J. 'Mutt' Summers, after which it went to Martlesham Heath for competitive trials. It was not a success, and nor were the designs from Supermarine's competitors. The Air Ministry were left with no alternative but to adopt the Gloster Gladiator, another biplane fighter.

Gunnery target

Despite the failure of the Supermarine entry Mitchell continued working on it, making improvements that included a retractable undercarriage and straight, thinner wings. With such refinements, he calculated that he could raise the F7/30's maximum speed to 265mph. This improved version was never built, but in concept it was much closer to the aircraft that would become the Spitfire. The original Type 224 F7/30 went to RAE Farnborough in 1935

Below: The first Spitfire, K5054. The aircraft featured a tail skid rather than a wheel. The shape of the fin and rudder was later altered.

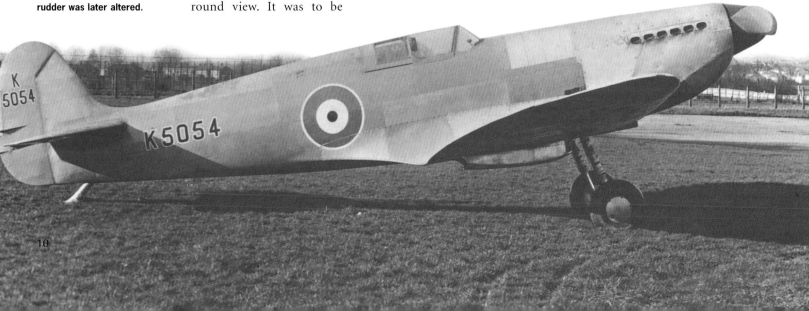

and from there back to Martlesham in 1937, eventually ending its days as a gunnery target on Orfordness ranges.

On 16 November 1934, the Air Ministry issued specification F5/34 in connection with the proposed monoplane fighter. Reginald Mitchell and his design team had already seen a draft of this specification in October, and at that time the Air Ministry suggested that it might be met by the revised F7/30 with a Napier Dagger engine, a proposal that was rejected. In November the Vickers-Supermarine Board, under the chairmanship of Sir Robert McLean, authorised Mitchell to proceed with an entirely new fighter design as a private venture. It was to be powered by the Rolls-Royce PV12, with Rolls-Royce contributing £7500 toward the cost of building a prototype.

On 1 December 1934, Supermarine received an Air Ministry contract for the redesigned fighter prototype, which was allocated the Company Type No 300. It was covered by specification F37/34; another specification, F36/34, covered a monoplane fighter design by Hawker, later to become the Hurricane.

Poetic

The aircraft that took shape on Mitchell's drawing board was a long way removed from the Type 224, even in its revised version. Whereas the latter had been angular in appearance, with a wing design resembling that of the Hurricane, the Type 300 could only be described as beautiful, its lines blending into one another in a way that was almost poetic. The wing was elliptical in plan, a shape that Mitchell had selected once before in a 1929 project for a six-engined flying boat.

It is not clear why Mitchell chose the elliptical shape. It was difficult to engineer, and calculations showed that it offered an aerodynamic performance at high speed less than one per cent better than a wing with a straight taper, but there is no doubt that it was successful. In the original design the wing was perfectly elliptical, but it was redesigned to produce the familiar Spitfire wing shape, with a greater flare to the curve of the trailing edge. The concept was not new. The Heinkel He 70, which had first flown in December 1932 and had been designed for high-speed communication and mail transport, had featured an elliptical wing; as did the early-model He 111 bomber.

Shrew and Shrike

The prototype Supermarine 300, which gradually took shape in the company's Woolston factory in the course of 1935, had yet to receive a name. Sir Robert McLean, chairman of Vickers-Supermarine, suggested that it should begin with 'S' and sound venomous. Shrew and Shrike had been suggested for the F7/30, and according to some sources so had Spitfire. McLean particularly liked the latter name, although neither Mitchell nor the Air Ministry did. Mitchell, in fact, is reported to have called it 'bloody silly'. But it stuck, and it was formally adopted after the Type 300's maiden flight.

Early in January 1936 the airframe of the Supermarine 300 was at last complete, having undergone a considerable number of modifications in its development phase. It was given the serial number K5054. The engine had been fitted the previous November, and all was set for the first flight. This took place on the morning of 5 March 1936, and 'Mutt' Summers was the pilot. The flight was made from Eastleigh airport and the Type 300, painted a pale blue-grey, took off 35 degrees across wind. This was because experience with the racing seaplanes had revealed a strong tendency to swing to port due to the high torque (the force exerted on the airframe by the rapid rotation of the propeller). Summers found that although there was indeed a tendency to swing, it was easily checked by the application of opposite rudder. The aircraft seemed to drift into the air, and the maiden flight, which was made with the undercarriage locked down, was effortless. When Summers landed, he told the Supermarine designers not to touch anything.

In fact, the only thing that was touched was the propeller. For the maiden flight K5054 had been fitted with a fine-pitch propeller to give the pilot more rpm and therefore more power on take-off. This propeller was replaced by a normal-pitch one for the second and subsequent flights, and Supermarine test pilots George Pickering and Jeffrey Quill joined Summers for the flying programme.

Gun platform

In addition to high power and refined aerodynamics, the other key factor was armament. The fighter aircraft had to be an effective gun platform. For 15 or more of the 20 years that separated the two world wars, the concept of the

Left: **This splendid Charles Brown photograph shows K9787, the first production Spitfire Mk I, flown here by Jeffrey Quill in May 1938. The Spitfire remained in production throughout WWII.**

Left: **This splendid Charles Brown photograph shows K9787, the first production Spitfire Mk I, flown here by Jeffrey Quill in May 1938. The Spitfire remained in production throughout WWII.**

traditional fighter layout died hard. In the early 1930s the world's leading air arms were still equipped with open-cockpit biplane or parasol-wing fighters, armed with two rifle-calibre machine guns mounted to fire through the propeller disc. The only large-calibre machine gun in general use in the later 1930s was the 12.7mm (0.50in) gun mounted in some American fighters and its 12.7mm or 13mm equivalents fitted in a few Continental designs like the Italian Fiat CR.32.

The problem of air armament was well summarized by Squadron Leader Ralph Sorley of Flying Operations 1 (FO1) in the British Air Ministry, leader of a campaign that led to the RAF's new monoplane fighters, the Spitfire and Hurricane, being fitted with eight 0.303in machine guns.

'The choice' (Sorley wrote later) 'lay between the 0.303 gun, the 0.50 gun and a new 20mm Hispano gun which was attracting the attention of the French, and in fact of other countries in Europe who could obtain knowledge of it from them.

During 1934 this gun was experimental and details of its performance and characteristics were hard to establish. On the other hand, designs of better 0.303 guns than the Vickers had been tested over the preceding years with the result that the American Browning from the Colt Automatic Weapon Corporation appeared to offer the best possibilities from the point of view of rate of fire. Our own development of guns of this calibre had been thorough but slow, since we were in the throes of economizing, and considerable stocks of old Vickers guns still remained from the first war. The acceptance of a new gun in the numbers likely to be required was a heavy financial and manufacturing commitment. The 0.50-inch on the other hand had developed little, and although it possessed a better hitting power the rate of fire was slow and it was a heavy item, together with its ammunition, in respect of installed weight...the controversy was something of a nightmare during 1933-34. It was a choice on which the whole concept of the fighter would depend, but a trial staged on the ground with eight 0.303s was sufficiently convincing and satisfying to enable them to carry the day.'

While the RAF opted for an armament of eight 0.303 guns (which would be replaced by four 20mm Hispano cannon from 1941) the Americans adopted a standard armament of up to six 0.50in guns in their new generation of monoplane fighters. The Germans, Italians, Russians, French and Japanese all settled for a mixed armament of cannon and machine guns, a pattern that would be maintained throughout much of World War II. But eight 0.303in guns packed a powerful punch; harmonized so that the bullets converged at 228m (250 yards), they could place a cone of fire into an area about 0.60m (2ft) in diameter at the rate of 8000 rounds per minute, a one-second burst hitting the target with a punishing 4.5kg (10lb) of metal.

Reflector gunsight

By September 1937 the Spitfire prototype K5054 had been fitted with its eight-gun armament and had been brought up to Spitfire Mk I production standards. Other refinements included the fitting of a Barr and Stroud Type GD5 reflector gunsight and a G22 camera gun. The original Rolls-Royce Merlin C engine had been replaced by a Merlin F, producing 780kW (1045hp). By this time the Spitfire was in full production, Supermarine having received an initial order for 310 aircraft on 3 June 1936. The first production Spitfire Mk I, serial number K9787, flew on 14 May 1938, and two days later it was delivered to No 19 Squadron at Duxford, Cambridgeshire – the first Spitfire to be taken on charge by RAF Fighter Command. Sadly, Reginald Mitchell never lived to see his creation in

RAF squadron colours. He died of cancer on 11 June 1937, only 42 years old – the disease had been diagnosed four years earlier. There is no doubt that Mitchell's refusal to rest while he was at work on the Spitfire design hastened his end. But before he died he was already at work on other projects, including the Type 317; a long-range, four-engined bomber.

Slow delivery

Because of the many problems associated with mass production, and the necessity of much sub-contracting, initial deliveries were slow, averaging only one aircraft per week. The other fighter squadron at Duxford, No 66, received its first Spitfire (K9802) on 31 October 1938. By the end of the year 45 aircraft had been delivered, which meant 19 and 66 Squadrons were at full strength. But the production schedule for the initial batch had slipped badly. It had been due for completion in March 1939, and was not fulfilled until August. As well as the problems of slow delivery, the Spitfire's introduction into service was marred by many accidents. Most of the pilots were used to flying fixed-undercarriage biplanes, and the transition to monoplanes with retractable landing gear, 100mph faster than their predecessors, was often not easy.

The initial order for 310 Spitfire Mk Is was followed by three more: two batches of 200 aircraft and one of 450. At the outbreak of war on 3 September 1939, nine RAF squadrons had fully rearmed with Spitfires and a tenth, No 609, was just beginning. In September No 603 Squadron, based at Turnhouse near Edinburgh, also began to receive Spitfires. It was the two Scottish Auxiliary Air Force squadrons, Nos 602 and 603, that were the first to make contact with the Luftwaffe over the United Kingdom.

Below: **K5054 looking somewhat sorry after a forced landing, caused by engine failure, during a test flight from Martlesham Heath on 22 March 1937. The pilot was Flying Officer Sam McKenna.**

CHAPTER TWO

Their Finest Hour:
The Battle of Britain

In October 1939 the Luftwaffe was fresh from its victories in Poland. But the Spitfire was to teach the German flyers the sharp lesson that daylight operations over the British Isles could not be carried out with impunity.

O n the morning of 16 October Junkers Ju 88 bombers of I/KG30 set out from Westerland, on the north German island of Sylt, to attack naval targets in the Firth of Forth. The Germans believed that the RAF had only a handful of Gloster Gladiator biplane fighters in the area, but they were wrong. The Spitfires of Nos 602 and 603 Squadrons were based at Drem and Turnhouse, while the Hurricanes of No 607 were at Usworth, near Sunderland, also in a position to cover the Firth. Two Ju 88s were shot down, one by Sqn Ldr E.E. Stevens of No 603 Squadron and the other by Flt Lt G. Pinkerton of No 602.

This was Fighter Command's first action of World War II. Although there had been plenty of false alarms in the first weeks of the war (one of which had ended in tragedy when Spitfires of No 74 Squadron shot down two Hurricanes in error in what became known as the 'Battle of Barking Creek'), the anticipated German bombing onslaught had not materialized. The Auxiliary Air Force squadrons in the north had several more encounters with the Luftwaffe in the weeks following 16 October, but it was not until 9 February 1940 that they scored their next success when a Heinkel He 111 was brought down near North Berwick by Sqn Ldr A.D. Farquhar of No 602 Squadron.

Prisoners

While the Scottish-based Spitfire squadrons carried out their primary task of defending the Royal Navy's bases during the first months of the war, those based south of the border, at Acklington in Northumberland and Catterick in North Yorkshire, also saw some early action. On 17 October 1939, three Spitfires of No 41 Squadron from Catterick caught a reconnaissance Heinkel He 111 25 miles off Whitby and shot it down into the sea. The pilot and navigator survived and were rescued from their dinghy at dawn the next day – the first German prisoners to be landed on English

Opposite: Spitfire Mk IIa of No 266 Squadron, RAF Hornchurch, Essex, in September 1940. This squadron operated Spitfires until the beginning of 1942, when it converted to Hawker Typhoons.

Below: Pilots of No 65 Squadron simulate a 'scramble' at RAF Hornchurch, Essex, in May 1939. The aircraft is a Spitfire Mk I.

Right: The Hawker Hurricane was the Spitfire's partner in the Battle of Britain. This photograph shows PZ865, the last Hurricane ever built, which featured in several films.

Below: This photograph of an armourer at work on the machine guns shows the Spitfire's elliptical wing shape to good advantage. The wing tips, secured by two bolts, could be detached.

soil in World War II. Although most of the enemy aircraft destroyed off north-east England during this phase fell to the Hurricanes of Nos 43 and 111 Squadrons, the Spitfires had their share. On 3 February 1940, for example, three Spitfire pilots of No 152 Squadron, Acklington, destroyed a Heinkel off the coast.

Lucky escape

One Spitfire pilot, Flt Lt Norman Ryder of No 41 Squadron, Catterick, had a very lucky escape. On 3 April 1940, Ryder shot down a Heinkel 111 between Redcar and Whitby, but his Spitfire was hit in the engine by return fire and he was forced to ditch in very rough seas close to a trawler. The impact with the water knocked him unconscious, and when he came to he was already some way below the surface in an aircraft that was sinking rapidly. He recalled later:

'I remember sitting in the cockpit and everything was a bright green. I was very fascinated by the stillness of it all – it was amazing, and I recall watching a lot of bubbles running up the windscreen before my nose and parting as they got to the front. I sat there fascinated by the sight and not a bit afraid. The calm was so restful after the noise. The green colour around me was lovely, but it turned to blackness before I got out. I started to get out by undoing my straps. I stood on my seat and just when I thought I was clear I found my parachute had caught under the sliding hood, and I could not move. I got partially into the cockpit again and at this point noticed that it was getting very much darker as the aircraft sank. I was again nearly hooked up by my parachute, but I wriggled and got clear. By now it was very black and I just saw the silhouette of the tailplane pass my face. I still had on my parachute which hampered my movement, but I managed to dog paddle my way upward.'

After considerable difficulty, Ryder freed himself from his parachute harness and, completely exhausted by his efforts, was picked up by the trawler crew. He had the dubious distinction of being the first Spitfire pilot to be shot down by the Luftwaffe, a fact compensated for to some extent by the award of the Distinguished Flying Cross.

Dunkirk battles

The first large-scale battles between the RAF's Spitfire and Hurricane squadrons and the Luftwaffe took place in May 1940, during the evacuation of the British Expeditionary Force from France via the port of Dunkirk. Since Dunkirk and the other ports were within easy reach of fighter bases in southern England, the German bombers could expect strong opposition. The Junkers Ju 87 Stuka dive-bombers, which were to suffer appalling losses in the Battle of Britain, had a foretaste of things to come on 25 May when a group of 15 of them were attacked by Spitfires over Calais and four were shot down. The day after that the Luftwaffe carried out its first major attacks on Dunkirk itself. Constant defensive patrols were maintained by 16 Spitfire and Hurricane squadrons of No 11 Group, RAF Fighter Command, whose pilots claimed 20 victories in the course of the day.

In the air battles that raged over and around the beaches during the nine days of the Dunkirk evacuation the RAF lost 177 aircraft, and the Luftwaffe sustained a comparable loss. Although these losses were roughly similar on paper, the fact was that the Luftwaffe had, for the first time, lost the air superiority it had enjoyed since its attack on Poland the year before. The British fighter pilots had dealt them a psychological blow – but an altogether more damaging one was to come in the skies over southern England before long.

Night combat

The defeat of France in June 1940 was followed by a growing number of incursions into British air space by enemy aircraft at night. Many of these raids were intercepted both by single-seater day fighters and by

Blenheim night fighters (the latter had already registered some successes as intruders during the Battle of France). At 0050 on 19 June, for example, Flt Lt R.M.B Duke-Woolley in a Blenheim of No 23 Squadron shot down a Heinkel He 111H-4 of 2/KG54 into the sea off the Norfolk coast. The German crew were captured. On the same night two Heinkels of 4/KG4 were also destroyed, both at 0115. Flt Lt A.G. ('Sailor') Malan in a Spitfire of No 74 Squadron destroyed the first off Felixstowe. The

Above: **Combat report submitted by Flt Lt A.G. 'Sailor' Malan on 19 June 1940. It describes a night combat with a Heinkel He 111; at that time the RAF had no dedicated night fighters.**

second was shot down jointly by a Spitfire of No 19 Squadron and a Blenheim of No 23 Squadron at Fleam Dyke, Cambridgeshire. Unfortunately the Spitfire pilot, Flying Officer Petra, was forced to bale out after his aircraft was hit; and the Blenheim pilot, Sqn Ldr O'Brien, baled out after losing control. Both the other Blenheim crew members were killed. Flying Officer G.E. Ball of No 19 Squadron, who shot down a Heinkel 111H of 6/KG4 into the sea off Margate, achieved the third victory of the night at 0215.

Three more Heinkels were destroyed in the early hours of 26 June. The first, a Heinkel He 111P-2 of 3/KG4, was shot down into the sea off Hull by Pilot Officers R.A. Smith and R. Marples at 0017, while two He 111H-3s of 3/KG26 were shot down by pilots of Nos 602 and 603 Squadrons off the Scottish coast. Interceptions like these were aided by the perfect visibility of the summer nights.

Convoy attacks

In June 1940, while the Battle of France still raged, the Luftwaffe began to turn its attention to 'fringe' targets, like ports on the English coast. This was a prelude to the larger-scale attacks that began early in July on shipping in the English Channel – the aim being to probe Fighter Command's defences and reaction times, and to tempt out and inflict damage on the British fighter squadrons. The convoy attacks continued through July and the first week of August.

Although there were several major air battles in this phase, mainly in the Dover area, the enemy formations were usually intercepted by only half a dozen British fighters, and were often able to carry out their attacks and head for home before any British fighters arrived. This was because Air Chief Marshal Sir Hugh Dowding, C-in-C Fighter Command, was husbanding his valuable fighter resources. He had earlier turned down repeated requests to send more RAF fighter squadrons to France, knowing that the decisive battle would be fought over the British Isles. The fighters available to him at the beginning of July 1940 numbered about 600 aircraft – 29 squadrons of Hurricanes, 19 of Spitfires, seven of Blenheim fighters (mostly assigned to night defence) and two of Boulton Paul Defiants. One of the Defiant squadrons, No 141, lost six aircraft in an encounter with Bf 109s on 19

Below: A bullet-riddled He 111 of KG26 in a field near Haddington, Lothian, Scotland, after being forced down by Spitfires of Nos 602 and 603 Squadrons on 29 November 1939.

Below: Harmonizing the guns of a 609 Sqn Spitfire. The fighter's eight machine guns could be aligned so that their cone of fire converged at a spot 220 yards ahead of the attacker.

July, and after that the Defiants played no further part in the daylight phase of the battle.

Dowding's approach was essentially a scientific one; he believed that Britain's air defences should have the benefit of the very latest technological developments. This was reflected in Fighter Command's operations rooms, linked with one another by an elaborate system of telephone and teleprinter lines to provide an integrated system of control. This enabled fighter aircraft to be passed rapidly from sector to sector and from group to group, wherever they were most needed. It was No 11 Group, in the crucial south-east of England, that would bear the brunt of the fighting throughout the battle; 29 of Dowding's squadrons were based there. Another 11 squadrons were in No 12 Group north of the Thames, and 17 in No 13 Group, covering northern England and Scotland.

Radar battle

Nowhere was modern technology more apparent in Britain's defences than in the use of radar, or radio direction finding (RDF) as it was then known. Developed by Robert Watson-Watt from earlier experiments in thunderstorm detection by the use of radio waves, the use of radar as an integral part of the British air defence system was largely the fruit of Dowding's initiative. He had worked with Watson-Watt in the 1930s and had quickly recognized the potential of the new invention. The Germans knew all

about the British radar warning system, and the destruction of the radar stations on the south coast of England was included in their plans as a necessary preliminary to the main air offensive against England.

Planning for the German offensive was completed by 2 August 1940. Air Fleets (Luftflotten) 2 and 3 were to attack simultaneously, their main tasks being to bring the RAF's fighters to combat, to destroy their airfields and the coastal radar stations, and to disrupt the RAF's ground organization in southern England. The attacks on the south coast radar stations began on 12 August. The station at Ventnor on the Isle of Wight was damaged beyond repair, but although others suffered damage they were operational again within hours. It turned out that the Germans did not fully understand the importance or the method of operation of the British radar, or its crucial value to the whole structure of the British air defence system. Attacks on radar sites were sporadic, and were soon abandoned – the Germans believed the radar sites' operations rooms were in bomb-proof underground bunkers and were therefore invulnerable. In fact, they were mostly in flimsy huts above ground.

Eagle attack

On 13 August 1940 the Luftwaffe launched the full weight of its air offensive against Britain with what they called the Adler Angriff (Eagle Attack). Its

Spitfire Mk I

initial objective was to neutralize RAF Fighter Command by striking at its airfields, and by drawing the fighter squadrons into combat. H-Hour at 0730 was postponed because of bad weather, but the Dornier Do 17s of KG2 failed to receive the order and set out over the Channel without fighter escort. They were attacked over the

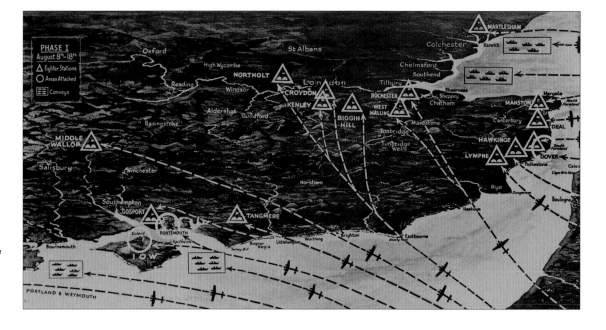

Right: Diagram showing the RAF airfield and merchant convoy targets assigned to the German Luftflotten at the beginning of the attack on England.

SPITFIRE Mk I

Type: single-seat interceptor fighter

Powerplant: one Rolls-Royce Merlin II or III rated at 1030hp (768Kw) at 16,250ft (4953m)

Performance: maximum speed 346mph (557km/h) at 15,500ft (4724m); maximum range 630 miles (1014km); range at maximum cruising speed 415 miles (668km); time to climb 6 minutes 51 seconds to 15,000ft (4572m); service ceiling 30,500ft (9296m)

Dimensions: span 36ft 10in (11.23m); length 29ft 11in (9.12m); height 12ft 8in (3.86m); wing area 242sq ft (22.48m²)

Below: A rather fanciful scoreboard displayed beside a Spitfire of No 92 (East India) Squadron in February 1941. Claims were almost always greatly exaggerated in the heat of battle.

Thames Estuary and five bombers were shot down, though the remainder caused heavy damage to Sheerness and Eastchurch. In the afternoon Ju 87s of Stukageschwader 2, escorted by Bf 109s of JG53, set out to attack airfields in the Portland area. They were engaged by Spitfires of No 609 Squadron and four Stukas were shot down. In all, the Luftwaffe lost 34 aircraft on 13 August. The RAF lost 12 Hurricanes, which had borne the brunt of the fighting, and one Spitfire.

Enemy attacks were disrupted by bad weather on 14 August, but the next day was to be the climax of the battle. Although 15 September, when heavy daylight attacks on London took place, was later designated as Battle of Britain Day, the heaviest fighting in fact took place on 15 August. It began in mid-morning, when 40 Stukas of Fliegerkorps II, escorted by a similar number of Bf 109s, were despatched to attack the airfields of Lympne and Hawkinge. The raid was intercepted over the coast by the Spitfires of No 54 and the Hurricanes of No 501 Squadrons, but while these took on the fighter escort, the Stukas broke through to hit Lympne, putting the airfield out of action for two days.

Attack on the north

At the same time aircraft of Luftflotte 5 from Norway and Denmark launched their first (and only) major daylight attack on the north of England. The two units involved, KG26 and KG30, had to fly 640 and 725km (400 and 450 miles) respectively from their bases at Stavanger and Aalborg to reach their targets on the north-east coast between Tyne and Humber. The first to approach over the North Sea were the 63 Heinkel 111s of KG26, escorted by 21 Messerschmitt Bf 110s of ZG76. 12 Spitfires of No 72 Squadron from Acklington intercepted them off the Farne Islands.

As it turned out, the size of the raid had been

Below: **Inside the cockpit of a Spitfire. The cockpit was small and compact, with the standard instrument panel as shown in the photograph.**

greatly underestimated by the British radar, which in fact had been tracking a formation of 20 He 115 seaplanes, sent towards the Firth of Forth as a diversion. The German plan had been to cross the north-east coast south of the Tyne and then fly south to their objectives, the airfields of Dishforth and Linton on Ouse, in Yorkshire. But the enemy had made a serious navigational error – they had made their landfall 100 miles too far north, and their track took them right across that of the diversionary seaplanes. So instead of the '30 plus' advised by radar, the 12 pilots of No 72 Squadron found themselves confronted with over 80 German aircraft.

Fortunately the Spitfires were quickly joined by the Hurricanes of No 79 Squadron, also from Acklington, and under the determined attacks of the two fighter squadrons the enemy formation was quickly disrupted. The bombers continued southwards, searching for their targets. The first wave, harried by the Hurricanes of 79 Squadron and some belonging to 605 Squadron, unloaded its bombs more or less at random between Newcastle and Sunderland. The second wave, attacked by the Spitfires of No 41 Squadron from Catterick and the Hurricanes of No 607 from Usworth, also dropped its load randomly and turned for home. Between them the two waves had lost eight Heinkels and six Bf 110s. The RAF lost only one aircraft, a 605 Squadron Hurricane which crashed while attempting a forced landing. The pilot was unhurt.

Meanwhile the 40 Ju 88s of KG30 were approaching the Yorkshire coast near Flamborough head. Radar detected them while they were still a long way out to sea, and Air Vice-Marshal Trafford Leigh-Mallory, commanding No 12 Group, ordered 18 Spitfires and Hurricanes of Nos 616 and 73 Squadrons up from Church Fenton to intercept them. Six Ju 88s were shot down, but the majority got through to the RAF airfield at Driffield, where their bombs destroyed four hangars and several Whitley bombers.

Southern battle

While the fighters of Nos 12 and 13 Groups were engaging Luftflotte 5 in the north-east, battle was joined again in the south. At 1500, a big radar plot began to build up as the Dornier 17s of KG3 assembled over their Belgian airfields and set course

over the Channel with a massive fighter escort of Bf 109s. Eleven fighter squadrons were scrambled to intercept, but such was the variety, number and complexity of the incoming raid plots that the fighters were shuttled to and fro by the sector controllers with no real co-ordination. KG3 broke through to bomb the airfields of Eastchurch and Rochester, and the fighter airfield at Martlesham Heath was heavily damaged by bomb-carrying Messerschmitts of Erprobungsgruppe 210 (a special unit which had been involved in

attacks on the south coast radar stations on 12 August) and put out of action for 36 hours.

Heavy losses

Two hours later, a mixed formation of Ju 87s and 88s of Luftflotte 2, again under heavy escort, took off from their airfields in the Cherbourg area. It took them a long time to assemble, and it was not until 1800 that the armada of 200 aircraft set course for the English coast. By then the Germans had thrown away their tactical advantage. The time that had elapsed since the earlier raids had enabled Air Vice-Marshals Keith Park and Quintin Brand (commanding 11 and 10 Groups respectively) to

Above: Spitfire Mk IIs in the final stages of assembly at the Castle Bromwich 'shadow factory', where all the Mk IIs were built. This photograph shows the sheer scale of the plant.

Below: Messerschmitt Bf 109Es of 8/JG2 Richthofen at an airfield in France, 1940. The Bf 109E was Fighter Command's principal opponent in the battle.

Right: A flight of Messerschmitt Bf 109s over the English Channel near Dover. Note the classic 'finger four' formation, developed by the Luftwaffe in the Spanish Civil War.

Below: Spitfire Mk Is of No 65 Squadron. The nearest aircraft is flown by Flying Officer (later Wing Commander) Robert Stanford Tuck, who became a noted wing leader in 1941.

take adequate counter-measures, and they were able to put up 14 fighter squadrons to meet the enemy assault. The Spitfires and Hurricanes engaged the bombers over the coast and concentrated on the Stukas, which were soon fighting for their survival. Other Spitfires pounced on the Ju 88s of Lehrgeschwader 1, which were trying to slip through to their targets, and inflicted heavy losses on them. Out of 15 aircraft of II/LG1, for example, only three managed to reach their objective, the Fleet Air Arm base at Worthy Down; the others were forced to jettison their bombs. The worst hit was IV/LG1, one flight of which lost five aircraft out of seven.

The day's fighting was by no means over. At 1935, 15 Bf 110s and eight Bf 109s of Erprobungsgruppe 210 set out to attack Kenley, south of London, but they made a navigational error and bombed Croydon by mistake, destroying 40 training aircraft. The Messerschmitts were engaged by the Hurricanes of Nos 32 and 111 Squadrons, and four Bf 110s were shot down. As the rest ran for the Channel, they were intercepted by the Spitfires of No 66 Squadron, which destroyed two more Bf 110s and a 109. This brought the Luftwaffe's combat losses for the day to 71 aircraft to the RAF's 30, of which 12 were Spitfires. The day's fighting had demonstrated that it was the Bf 109 that was causing the Spitfire and Hurricane squadrons their biggest problems. The twin-engined Bf 110 'Destroyer', intended as a long-range escort fighter, had shown itself markedly inferior to the British fighters, and no fewer than 31 had been destroyed in the course of the day. The Bf 110 would continue to suffer unacceptable losses throughout the battle.

Brief respite

Although the Germans struck hard at eight RAF airfields in the morning of 16 August, in the afternoon bad weather frustrated the Luftwaffe's attempts to make further attacks. Nevertheless, air combats that day, mostly in the morning, cost the Luftwaffe 44 aircraft and the RAF 26, 11 of them Spitfires. Five of the downed Spitfires were from No 266 Squadron from Hornchurch, 'bounced' by Bf 109s over Canterbury.

Poor weather again prevailed on 17 August, bringing a brief respite for the hard-pressed RAF fighter squadrons, but on the 18th the Luftwaffe launched a series of heavy attacks on the important sector stations of Kenley and Biggin Hill. Kenley was badly hit, and its operations room was put out of action. In the afternoon a strong force of Stukas attacked the airfields at Ford, Gosport and Thorney Island without adequate fighter

escort. They were engaged by the Hurricanes of No 43 and the Spitfires of Nos 152 and 602 Squadrons, and 18 Stukas were destroyed. The Luftwaffe lost 60 aircraft in the day's fighting, the RAF 34. The Hurricane squadrons had taken a terrible mauling, losing 29 fighters, some in airfield attacks, with 13 more damaged. The Spitfire squadrons escaped relatively lightly, with five aircraft destroyed and 14 damaged.

Defensive shield

The weather improved steadily in the last week of August, and the Luftwaffe stepped up its airfield attacks, striking hard at the fighter bases that formed a defensive shield around London. The attacks were to last for two weeks, and marked a crucial phase in the battle. Both sides had used the bad weather to recoup their strength. The Germans moved the fighters of Luftflotte 3 to reinforce those of Luftflotte 2 in the Pas de Calais, while the RAF took delivery of replacement fighters – including 60 much-needed Spitfires in the period 19–24 August.

Most of these new Spitfires were Mk IIs, produced by the Nuffield factory at Castle Bromwich. The differences between the Mk I and Mk II were minor, the principal one being that the Mk II had a Merlin XII engine that

Below: **Spitfire Mk Is of No 19 Squadron, the first unit to receive the type, pictured at RAF Duxford before the outbreak of World War II.**

ran on 100 octane fuel and used a Coffman cartridge starter instead of a trolley-accumulator. The Mk II also had 33kg (73lb) of armour plate fitted on the production line, whereas the Mk I's armour had been fitted retrospectively in service. Other modifications included bullet-proof windscreens, not fitted previously. Dowding famously commented that, if Chicago gangsters could protect themselves with bullet-proof glass, his pilots should too.

Exhaustion

The replacements came just in time, for losses were beginning to mount. Six Spitfires were lost on 24 August and eight on the 25th; and on the following day No 616 Squadron, in the thick of the fighting, lost no fewer than seven Spitfires – though five of the pilots were saved. By mid-week, every squadron in No 11 Group was suffering seriously from exhaustion. Some units were down to half strength, and they had to be withdrawn from the battle and sent north into No 13 Group's area for a rest. On 30 August, the vital sector station of Biggin Hill was completely wrecked by bombing, and it was attacked again the following

afternoon, along with Hornchurch. Fighter Command lost 11 Spitfires on the 30th, and 14 more on the 31st. Three of these belonged to No 19 Squadron, which had been carrying out trials with 20mm cannon with little success.

Losses

Of the 328 Spitfires delivered to Fighter Command since the beginning of July, 163 had been destroyed and 161 damaged, though the latter were repairable. As yet, the squadrons of No 12 Group north of the Thames had not been committed in strength to the battle, but of necessity that would soon change. Fighter Command's situation was now very serious indeed. In the space of the fortnight from 24 August to 6 September the RAF lost 103 pilots killed and 128 badly wounded – this represented almost a quarter of the available trained fighter pilots. Maintaining the flow of replacement pilots was becoming a serious problem. Some were being sent to front line squadrons with as little as 20 hours' flying experience on Spitfires and Hurricanes, and many of the fighter pilots joining their squadrons early in

Below: **Spitfire Mk IIa of the Battle of Britain Memorial Flight pictured at Duxford during the annual Battle of Britain Air Display.**

Left: Polish pilots of No 303 'Kosciusko' Squadron, which operated from Northolt in the Battle of Britain from the beginning of August until October.

September 1940 did not survive their first sortie, such was their lack of experience. Others managed to hang on and found themselves catapulted from the lowly status of new boys to section and even flight commanders in record time.

By 3 September, for the first time in the battle, Luftwaffe crews were returning to base and reporting that they had encountered no opposition. It was beginning to look as if the collapse of Fighter Command were imminent. But a chain of events was about to bring a dramatic and unexpected change in enemy policy. On the night of 24 August, a few German bombers made a navigational error and dropped some bombs on London, and on the following night RAF Bomber Command retaliated by attacking Berlin. Provoked by this, Hitler pressed the Luftwaffe C-in-C, Hermann Göring, to switch the main bombing offensive away from the airfields, to London. This plan was bitterly opposed by General Hugo Sperrle, commanding Luftflotte 3, who believed (probably rightly) that if the airfield attacks were kept up for another few days the Luftwaffe would

achieve air superiority over south England, opening up the possibility of an invasion.

Safer bases

On the other hand, the Luftflotte 2 commander, General Albert Kesselring, thought that the RAF

Below: Spitfire Mk IA R6800 of No 66 Squadron at Gravesend. This aircraft was shot down by the German ace Werner Mölders on 17 October 1940.

Above: Pilots of No 610 Squadron, Biggin Hill, at readiness in September 1940. No 610 Squadron, an Auxiliary Air Force unit, operated Spitfires throughout the war.

was about to evacuate its fighters from the hard-hit 11 Group airfields and withdraw them to safer bases to the north and west of London, out of range of the German fighter escorts. His belief was that an all-out assault on London would force the RAF to throw its last fighter reserves into the defence of the capital. Göring was persuaded by Kesselring's argument, and the attacks on London were authorized. Meanwhile on 5 September, 22 German bomber formations attacked RAF airfields and the oil storage tanks at Thameshaven, the Luftwaffe losing 23 aircraft and Fighter Command 20. For once, Spitfire losses exceeded Hurricanes by 13 aircraft to seven. About a third of these were suffered by No 41 Squadron, which had recently arrived in the combat area from Catterick. The heaviest combat losses in this period were sustained by squadrons newly rotated back to 11 Group after

being rested elsewhere – another indication of the vulnerability of the replacement pilots.

Bitter combats

The Thameshaven attack was a prelude to the main assault on London, which began at 1500 on 7 September and lasted throughout the night. The London docks were pounded by 625 bombers, escorted in the daylight hours by 617 fighters. The civilian death toll was 448, with many more injured, and the severity of the attacks was such that the codeword Cromwell – signifying 'invasion imminent' – brought the British defences to their highest level of readiness. Of the 23 RAF fighters lost in the bitter combats of 7 September, eight were Spitfires. The Luftwaffe lost 38 aircraft.

The attacks continued and on 11 September, for the first time, the RAF suffered more heavily than the Luftwaffe, losing 27 aircraft to 22. Eight Spitfires were destroyed and ten damaged. After a spell of bad weather, eight more Spitfires were destroyed on 14 September. Then on 15 September the Luftwaffe threw 200 bombers against London in two waves. When the first wave attacked, the RAF had no more fighter squadrons in reserve; if the second wave had come immediately, the Spitfires and Hurricanes would have been caught on the ground as they refuelled and rearmed, allowing the enemy to bomb without opposition. But it was two hours before the second wave attacked, and by that time the fighter squadrons were once more ready for it. A total of 148 bombers got through to attack London, but 56 were shot down and many more limped back to their bases with severe battle damage. To the Luftwaffe, 15 September was remembered as 'Black Sunday'. Fighter Command's loss was 29, of which 22 were Hurricanes – once again, the Spitfire squadrons had escaped comparatively lightly.

Towards the end of September, dense cloud cover stretched over much of the British Isles, and the Luftwaffe's tactics underwent a complete change. The large daylight formations were abandoned. Instead the Luftwaffe began to send over small groups of aircraft, including bomb-carrying Messerschmitts, at high altitude. The Luftwaffe had clearly failed to achieve its objectives in daylight, but from the beginning of November it began to step up its night attacks on London and other targets. The Battle of Britain had ended in victory for Fighter Command, but the ordeal of

Britain's cities was only just beginning.

Of the 742 Spitfires delivered to the RAF between 1 July and 31 October 1940, 361 were lost and 352 damaged. In the same period, 565 Hurricanes were lost and 455 damaged.

The importance of the Luftwaffe's failure over Britain rests in the fact that the island could later be used as a base for the Allied air offensive against Germany and for the Allied invasion of the European continent, which decided the war in the West. But it was fighter strength that decided the Battle of Britain – that, and the sacrifice of 537 young fighter pilots. The two fighter aircraft they flew, the Spitfire and the Hurricane, both became immortal in the heart of the British nation; but it was the Spitfire that became the legend.

Above: 'The swirling vortex of invisible battle'; a dogfight in progress over Maidstone, Kent. Pilots, as yet, had no idea what caused condensation trails.

Below: The sole Spitfire Mk III, intended as an air superiority fighter, saw a good deal of experimental flying and yielded much information which was used in the design of later marks.

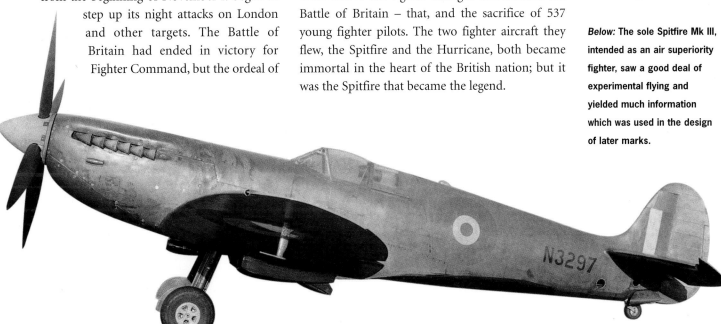

CHAPTER THREE

In Action Over Northwest Europe, 1941–43

The Battle of Britain was over. Hitler had postponed indefinitely the plan for the invasion of Britain, Operation Sea Lion, and it was time for RAF Fighter Command to turn from defence to attack. On 20 December 1940 two Spitfires of No 66 Squadron, flown by Flight Lieutenant G.P. Christie and Pilot Officer C.A.W. Brodie, took off from Biggin Hill and set course across the Channel under a low cloud base. Crossing the enemy coast at Dieppe, they swept down on Le Touquet airfield and strafed several installations. There was no opposition from either flak or fighters, and both Spitfires returned safely to base.

Opposite: A splendid Charles Brown photograph of a Spitfire Mk V of No 222 Squadron, which operated this mark from North Weald in 1941. The squadron converted to Hawker Tempests late in 1944.

Below: Spitfire Mk VB AB910 of the Battle of Britain Memorial Flight, seen in the markings of No 92 Squadron. During WWII, this aircraft made one circuit of an airfield with a WAAF hanging on its tail; she survived.

Over the next few days Spitfires and Hurricanes from various squadrons, operating in twos and threes, made short forays into enemy territory, again without meeting opposition. Encouraged, Fighter Command decided to try something bigger, and on 9 January 1941, in brilliant sunshine and perfect visibility, five fighter squadrons penetrated 50km (30 miles) into France. There was no sign of enemy movement, either on the ground or in the air. The next morning, six Blenheims of No 114 Squadron, escorted by six squadrons of Spitfires and Hurricanes, attacked ammunition and stores dumps in the Forêt de Guines. A few enemy fighters were encountered and there was some skirmishing, in the course of which one Hurricane was shot down. Two battle-damaged Spitfires crash-landed on return to base, and one of the pilots was killed. It was an inauspicious end to the RAF's first combined daylight bombing raid and fighter sweep, known as Circus No 1. Nevertheless, offensive sweeps were carried out whenever the weather permitted during the early weeks of 1941, and Luftwaffe opposition gradually increased.

Spitfire V

By March 1941, fighter sweeps over the Continent were becoming tightly-organized affairs, with the Spitfire and Hurricane squadrons operating at wing strength. A Fighter Command wing consisted of three squadrons, each of 12 aircraft. There were Spitfire wings at Biggin Hill, Hornchurch and Tangmere, mixed Spitfire and Hurricane wings at Duxford, Middle Wallop and Wittering, and Hurricane wings at Kenley, Northolt and North Weald. The Hurricane wings would soon be rearmed with Mk V Spitfires, which first came into service that same March.

Converted from the Mk I airframe, the Mk V was to be the main production version of the

Spitfire. 6479 Mk V Spitfires were built in total. The majority of Spitfire Vs were armed with two 20mm cannon and four machine guns, packing a more powerful punch, particularly against armour plating. The Mk V was powered by a Rolls-Royce Merlin 45 engine, developing 1056kW (1415hp) at 5000m (16,400ft) compared with the 858kW (1150hp) of the Merlin XII fitted in the Mk II.

But the Mk V was essentially a compromise aircraft, rushed into service to meet an urgent requirement for a fighter with a performance superior to that of the latest model of Messerschmitt – the Bf 109F. The debut of the Spitfire V came just in time, because the Bf 109F began to arrive with the Luftwaffe fighter units in May 1941 (the new Messerschmitt had suffered from technical problems in its development phase, but these had now been resolved). On 11 May, a

Below: **A neat formation of Spitfire IXs of No 611 Squadron, RAF Biggin Hill, photographed early in 1943. Note the wing blisters over the 20mm cannon breeches.**

group of bomb-carrying Bf 109Fs attacked Lympne and Hawkinge, one being shot down by a Spitfire. But the Spitfire V failed to deliver the overall superiority Fighter Command needed so badly. At high altitude, where a high proportion of the decisive combats took place, it was found to be inferior to the Bf 109F on most counts, and several squadrons equipped with the Mk V took a severe mauling during that summer.

'Sailor' Malan

In the spring and summer of 1941 the Biggin Hill Wing was made up by Nos 72, 92 and 609 Squadrons, all of which had achieved impressive records in the Battle of Britain. It was led by Wing Commander A.G. Malan, a South African with 18 confirmed victories, a DSO and two DFCs. Known by his nickname of 'Sailor' because of his pre-war service in the Merchant Navy, he was one of the RAF's foremost air combat tacticians, and his famous 'Ten Rules of Air Fighting' were displayed on dispersal hut walls throughout Fighter Command.

The pilots of the Biggin Hill Wing were proud to belong to what was generally regarded as an elite formation. One of them was Sergeant (later Flight Lieutenant) Jim Rosser of No 72 Squadron, who flew his first fighter sweeps in the spring of 1941. One of his early experiences was typical:

'We would cross the Channel in sections, line astern, climbing all the time. We always climbed into the sun, which was absolute hell; your eyes felt as though they were burning down into your head

and within a few minutes you were saturated in sweat. I will never forget my first operation; 72 Squadron was flying top cover and I was "Yellow Two", in other words the number two aircraft in Yellow Section. Quite honestly, I hadn't a clue what was going on. We flew a sort of semi-circle over France, still in sections line astern, and then came out again. I never saw a single enemy aircraft, but we must have been attacked, because when we got home three of our Spits were missing.'

Seven 109s

No 72 Squadron's commanding officer was an Australian, Squadron Leader Desmond Sheen, who had begun his operational career with the squadron

Above: Spitfire Vs of No 485 (New Zealand) Squadron, formed at Driffield, Yorkshire, in March 1941. It later converted to Typhoons.

Below: Spitfire VB of No 316 (Warszawski) Squadron, a Polish unit formed at Pembrey, Wales, in February 1941. It was originally armed with Hurricanes.

before the war. In April 1940 he had been posted to No 212 Squadron (the only Spitfire squadron to operate from French soil during the Battle of France) and in the next few weeks he flew photo-reconnaissance sorties all over Europe in specially-modified Spitfires, returning to No 72 Squadron just in time to take part in the Battle of Britain.

Sheen was to lead the squadron in sweeps over occupied Europe for eight months, from March to November 1941. Sheen's opposite number in No 92 Squadron was Squadron Leader Jamie Rankin, a Scot from Portobello, Edinburgh, who had originally joined the Fleet Air Arm but later transferred to the RAF. When he was appointed to command No 92 Squadron in March 1941 it was the top-scoring unit in Fighter Command, and its score steadily increased under Rankin's leadership. Rankin himself opened his score with No 92 by destroying a Heinkel He 59 floatplane and damaging a Bf 109 on 11 April. This was followed by another confirmed 109 on the 24th, and in June, a month of hectic air fighting over France, he shot down seven more 109s and claimed another probably destroyed.

Douglas Bader

Douglas Bader commanded the Tangmere Wing (Nos 145, 610 and 616 Squadrons, all flying Spitfire Vs). Bader's reputation was near-legendary, partly because he flew with artificial legs as the result of a pre-war flying accident. By the end of July 1941 his personal score stood at 22 enemy aircraft destroyed. He had an aversion to cannon armament, believing

Below: Ground crew rearming and refuelling a Spitfire under simulated gas attack conditions. Poison gas was considered a credible threat.

that it encouraged pilots to open fire at too great a range, so his personal aircraft was a Spitfire VA with an armament of eight machine guns.

Handling the large fighter formations that were being pushed across the Channel in the summer of 1941 called for a high level of skill on the part of the controllers. By July 1941 Circus operations were very large affairs, with as many as 18 squadrons of fighters covering a small force of bombers. Getting six wings of Spitfires airborne, to the rendezvous at the right time and place, and shepherding them into and out of enemy territory, was something of a nightmare for everyone concerned. It began on the ground. Three squadrons of Spitfires – 36 aircraft – made an impressive sight as they taxied round the perimeter of an airfield, but with propellers revolving dangerously close to wingtips and tails it was all too easy to make a mistake. A late starter would add to the problems as the pilot edged around the outside of the queue, trying to catch up with the rest of his squadron.

The rendezvous with the bombers, usually over Manston, was another critical moment. A Spitfire's tanks held only 85 gallons of petrol, and every minute spent in waiting for the Blenheims to turn up reduced a pilot's chances of getting home safely if he found himself in trouble over France. Over enemy territory the Luftwaffe always seemed to have the advantage. No matter how high the Spitfires climbed, the 109s usually managed to climb higher, ready to pounce on the 'tail-end Charlies' of the fighter formations and pick them off. There was no dog-fighting in the original sense of the word; the Messerschmitts fought on the climb and dive, avoiding turning combat with the more manoeuvrable Spitfires wherever possible. The difference between life and death was measured in mere seconds.

Biggest sweep

One of the biggest fighter sweeps of 1941, Circus 62, was mounted on 7 August, when 18 squadrons of Spitfires and two of Hurricanes accompanied six Blenheim bombers in an attack on a power station at Lille. The whole force made rendezvous over Manston, with the North Weald Wing (made up of the Hurricanes of No 71 Squadron and the Spitfires of Nos 111 and 222 Squadrons) providing close support for the bombers. Behind and above, as

Armour Protection

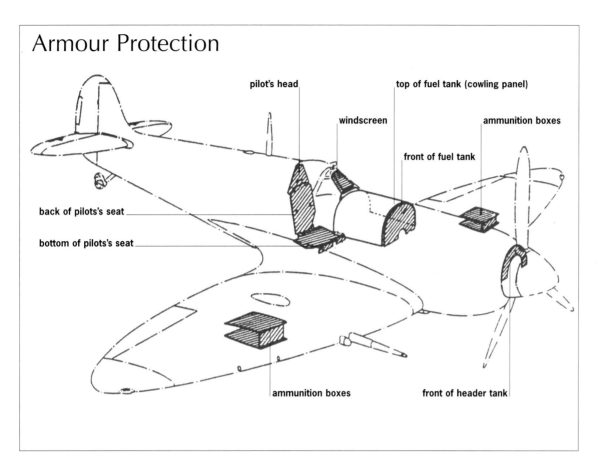

pilot's head

windscreen

top of fuel tank (cowling panel)

ammunition boxes

front of fuel tank

back of pilots's seat

bottom of pilots's seat

ammunition boxes

front of header tank

Left: Diagram showing the position of the armour protection in a Spitfire VB. Spitfires did not have bullet-proof windscreens until the Battle of Britain.

immediate top cover, came the three Spitfire squadrons of the Kenley Wing: Nos 452 (Australia), 485 (New Zealand), and 602. High above this 'beehive' of nearly 80 fighters and bombers came the three target support wings, flying at 8200m (27,000ft). They were the Biggin Hill Wing, with Nos 72, 92 and 609 Squadrons; the Hornchurch Wing, with Nos 403 (Canadian), 603 and 511 Squadrons; and Douglas Bader's Tangmere Wing, with Nos 41, 610 and 616 Squadrons. The target support force's task was to assure air superiority over and around Lille while the attack was in progress.

On this occasion, however, the Luftwaffe refused to be drawn into battle in large numbers. Six weeks earlier, the Germans had invaded the Soviet Union, and many fighter units had been transferred from the Channel area to the Eastern Front. Those that remained, seriously outnumbered in the face of Fighter Command's growing strength, had been ordered to conserve their resources. The 109s stayed well above the Spitfire formations, shadowing them. From time to time, small numbers of Messerschmitts broke away, darting down to fire on a straggler, always disengaging when the rest of the

Spitfires turned on them. The 109s shot down one of No 41 Squadron's flight commanders in this way.

The bombers meanwhile had found Lille obscured by cloud, so had turned back towards the Channel to attack a concentration of barges at Gravelines. A fierce air battle was already in progress over the coast, where two Polish squadrons of the Northolt Wing, Nos 306 and 308, had been waiting

Below: His Majesty King George V examining the cockpit of a Spitfire. King George and Queen Elizabeth made frequent visits to RAF bases.

Right: Spitfire VBs of No 243 Squadron over northern England in the summer of 1942. The squadron left for North Africa in November.

to cover the Blenheims during the final phase of their withdrawal. 308 Squadron was suddenly bounced by about 18 Messerschmitts, and lost two Spitfires. The Blenheims made their escape, but the rear support wing, comprising Nos 19, 257 and 401 Squadrons, was attacked and lost two Spitfires and a Hurricane. The RAF had therefore lost six aircraft, an outcome which, set against a claim of three Bf 109s destroyed, could hardly be considered favourable.

Right: The type of gyro gunsight fitted to a Spitfire. The switch could be turned so that an illuminated graticule corresponded with the wingspan of an enemy aircraft type.

Isolated

Another large operation, Circus 63, was mounted two days later on Saturday 9 August. This time the Blenheims' objective was a supply dump in the Béthune area. Once again, Bader's Tangmere Wing formed part of the target support force, but things went wrong from the start when No 41 Squadron failed to rendezvous on time. The remainder, unable to wait, carried on across the Channel. For a while all was peaceful; then just a few miles short of the target, the 109s hit them hard. Bader's pilots were hard put to hold their own, the wing becoming badly dislocated as the Messerschmitts pressed home determined attacks. Bader himself misjudged an attack on a 109 and found himself isolated. Six enemy fighters closed in on him but by superb flying he destroyed two. The end came soon afterwards, when another 109 collided with him and severed his Spitfire's fuselage just behind the cockpit. Bader managed to struggle clear of the plunging aircraft, leaving one of his artificial legs still trapped inside. His parachute opened, and he floated down to a painful landing and captivity.

As August gave way to September, some senior Air Staff officers began to have serious doubts about the value of Circus operations. Fighter Command losses were climbing steadily, and the results achieved hardly seemed to justify them. The new

AOC of 11 Group, Air Vice-Marshal Trafford Leigh-Mallory, claimed that between 14 June and 3 September 1941 his pilots had destroyed 437 German fighters, with another 182 'probables'. As the Luftwaffe never had more than 260 single-engined fighters in France and the Low Countries at any one time during this period, this claim later proved to be wildly exaggerated – the actual figure was 128 destroyed and 76 damaged. Fighter Command lost 194 pilots in those three months. The RAF's claim for the six and a half months from 14 June to 31 December 1941, 731 enemy aircraft destroyed, was equally exaggerated. The actual German loss was 154, including 51 not attributable to combat. Fighter Command's losses came to 411.

Focke-Wulf 190

A growing proportion of the RAF's losses were attributable to a single new factor. In September 1941, Polish pilots of No 315 Squadron, returning to base after Circus 101, reported being attacked by 'an unknown enemy aircraft with a radial engine'. RAF Intelligence concluded correctly that the Luftwaffe's latest fighter, the Focke-Wulf 190, had arrived in France. The first unit to receive the aircraft on the Channel coast was Jagdgeschwader 26, closely followed by JG2, and by October 1941 the RAF were running into more and more of them. Within weeks, the Fw 190 had established air superiority east of the Channel, outclassing the Spitfire VB at all altitudes and in every respect except radius of turn. On the personal orders of Winston Churchill, Fighter Command's sweeps over France were halted in November. No 118 Squadron, flying Spitfire VBs from Ibsley, participated in one of the last, flown on 15 November 1941. The Squadron War Diary tells the story:

'It was decided in the afternoon to carry out a most ill-conceived scheme, designated Rodeo 5, in which the Middle Wallop Wing rendezvoused with the Whirlwinds of 263 Squadron and carried out a sweep of the Channel Islands area.' (No 263 was one of two squadrons equipped with the twin-engined Westland Whirlwind, armed with four 20mm cannon. Designed as a long-range escort fighter, it was later used as a fighter-bomber.) 'The whole sortie seems to have been one long muddle. The Whirlwinds led the Spits much too far south and

Below: **The Focke-Wulf Fw 190 was the Spitfire's most formidable opponent. Seen here is an Fw 190A of JG54.**

Right: Close-up of the nose of a Spitfire Mk IXLF, showing the Merlin 66 engine and Rotol four-bladed propeller, stripped of its spinner.

Right: Close-up of the nose of a Spitfire Mk IXLF, showing the Merlin 66 engine and Rotol four-bladed propeller, stripped of its spinner.

Below: The first high-altitude Spitfire Mk VI, fitted with a pressurized cockpit and a Merlin 47 engine, seen at Hucknall. Note the extended wingtips.

then returned right over the flak area. 501 Squadron were sent out to deal with a few Huns that put in an appearance when we were on the way back. 118 went back to help, but 501 were not located. The net result was at least three planes damaged by flak and enemy aircraft, and one shot down, and all we could claim was one enemy aircraft damaged.'

Mk IX

Meanwhile, development of the Spitfire design had been moving forward. To counter the activities of high-flying German reconnaissance aircraft the Spitfire Mk VI was produced, with a long, tapered wing and a pressurized cockpit; the aircraft was assigned to a specialized flight of a home defence squadron. The Mk VII, also with a pressurized cockpit, was powered by a Rolls-Royce Merlin 60 engine, a two-stage, two-speed, inter-cooled powerplant that took the development of the Merlin to its ultimate level of performance. Early in 1942, Air Staff were intending to produce both the Spitfire Mk VII and the Spitfire Mk VIII (in much larger numbers). The Mk VIII was to be an unpressurized version of the Mk VII, intended for low-level air superiority operations as a counter to the Fw 190.

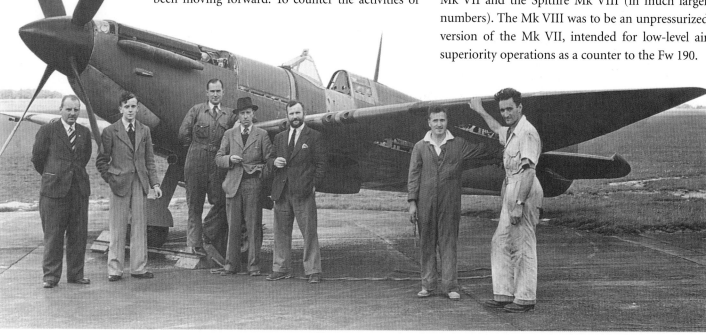

But the Mk VIII design needed a lot of refinement, including a general strengthening of the fuselage, which meant that production would be delayed for an unacceptably long time. The Air Staff therefore turned to an interim solution: a Mk V Spitfire airframe combined with a Merlin 61 engine. The resulting combination was the Spitfire Mk IX, which for a stop-gap aircraft turned out to be a resounding success. Deliveries to the RAF began in June 1942 and 5665 were built, more than any other version apart from the Mk V.

Circus resumed

Meanwhile by March 1942 Circus operations had been resumed, albeit on a reduced scale. The vulnerable Blenheims of Bomber Command's No 2 Group were replaced by the faster, more modern Douglas Boston. The number of Bostons involved in these operations was never more than 30 but they were often escorted by up to 27 squadrons of Spitfires, nearly half Fighter Command's available strength. On one occasion, on 30 April 1942, no fewer than 38 squadrons of Spitfires were involved in escorting 24 Bostons on four separate operations. Only six Bostons were lost in April but Spitfire losses were heavy as the Fw 190s (and, to a lesser extent, the Bf 109Fs) continued to show their

superiority over the Spitfire V. For example, 11 Spitfires failed to return on 4 April, 15 on 12 April, and 12 on 25 April. Spitfire losses for the whole of the month were 59 aircraft.

The sternest test for Fighter Command in 1942 was the Dieppe operation of 19 August (Operation Jubilee), one object of which was to bring to battle all the forces of the Luftwaffe in northern France and the Low Countries. Control of the RAF part of the operation was given to Air Vice-Marshal Trafford Leigh-Mallory of No 11 Group. 56 squadrons of Spitfires, Hurricanes and Typhoons were placed at his disposal, as well as five Blenheim and Boston squadrons of No 2 Group and four Mustang squadrons of Army Co-operation Command. The story of that ill-fated venture, and of the gallantry of the Canadian troops who suffered appalling casualties in the landing, is well known. Dieppe was a disaster for the RAF, too – in the day's operations the RAF lost 106 aircraft to the Luftwaffe's 48. Of the RAF losses, 88 were fighters, and the majority were Spitfires.

American Eagles

Tuesday 29 September 1942 was a significant day for the officers and men of Nos 71, 121 and 133 Spitfire Squadrons. Known as the Eagle Squadrons,

Below: **Spitfire Mk IX in the markings of No 316 (Polish) Squadron. The code SZ was carried by this squadron from February 1941 until December 1946, when it disbanded.**

these three units had been formed from a nucleus of American volunteer pilots in 1940–41. Now based together at Debden in Essex, they were formally handed over to VIII Fighter Command, United States Army Air Force to become the 334th, 335th and 336th Fighter Squadrons of the 4th Fighter Group. From now on the primary task of the pilots would be bomber escort to the Boeing B-17s that had become operational with the Eighth AAF in the United Kingdom that summer. The pilots of No 133 Squadron had already had an unfortunate taste of this type of mission on 4 September, when 12 brand new Spitfire IXs accompanied a formation of B-17 Fortresses in an attack on Morlaix. A serious

navigational error, compounded by bad weather, had resulted in 11 of the 12 Spitfires running out of fuel over the Brest peninsula on the return flight. Four pilots were killed, and the rest were taken prisoner. The 4th Fighter Group continued to fly Spitfires until March 1943, when it rearmed with Republic P-47 Thunderbolts.

Escort missions

The following extract from the War Diary of No 118 Squadron, flying its Spitfire VBs from Coltishall in Lincolnshire, well illustrates the typical activity of a Spitfire squadron early in 1943. It describes an operation flown on 21 January:

Below: **Pilots of the 4th Fighter Group, USAAF, scramble for the benefit of the press at Debden in 1942. The 4th FG exchanged its Spitfires for P-47s in March 1943.**

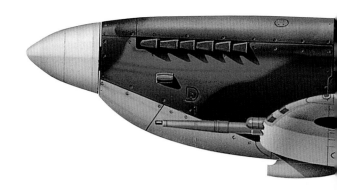

Spitfire Mk IX

SPITFIRE Mk IX

Type: fighter

Powerplant: one 1565hp Rolls-Royce Merlin 61 or 1650hp Merlin 63 12-cylinder V-type

Max speed: 655km/h (408mph) at 7320m (24,000ft)

Service ceiling: 12,105m (43,000ft)

Max range: 1576km (980 miles)

Wing span: 11.23m (36ft 10in)

Length: 9.46m (31ft)

Height: 3.85m (12ft 7¾in)

Weights: empty 2545kg (5610lb); max take-off 4309kg (9500lb)

Armament: two 20mm cannon and four 7.7mm (0.303in) MG (Mk IXe)

Left: Comforts for the troops: a Spitfire Mk IXE en route to Normandy with two 18-gallon (81-litre) beer barrels attached to its underwing shackles.

'Misery (the Squadron Intelligence Officer) went on a 48 (hours' leave) and of course things happened: there were four flights by 27 aircraft in fine weather. In the morning there was drogue towing, air-to-air and air-to-sea firing, camera gun practice, camera tests and in the afternoon a sweep over Ijmuiden... In the afternoon the Squadron made rendezvous with 167' (another Spitfire V squadron, whose personnel were mainly Dutch) 'and 12 Venturas over Mundesley and flew at sea level to within a few miles of the Dutch coast, then climbed to 9000ft over Ijmuiden. As we crossed the coast four Fw 190s were seen breaking cloud below at 2000 feet. Our allotted task was to give top cover to the bombers which, instead of bombing immediately, went inland for ten minutes then turned round and bombed from east to west on an outward heading. Squadron Leader Wooton decided not to go down for the 190s until the bombers had carried out their task, or while they were still in danger of being attacked. While the bombers and escorts were making their manoeuvre the 190s climbed up and were joined by others, but before they could attack the bombers 118 Squadron engaged them. In the following dog-fight, of which no one seemed to have a very clear picture, Sgt Lack destroyed a Fw 190 which he followed down to sea level and set on fire; it was eventually seen to crash into the sea by (Sgt) Hallingworth.

'Hallingworth was attacked and his aircraft hit, and he in turn claimed a 190 damaged. The CO, who engaged the leading Fw 190, also claimed one

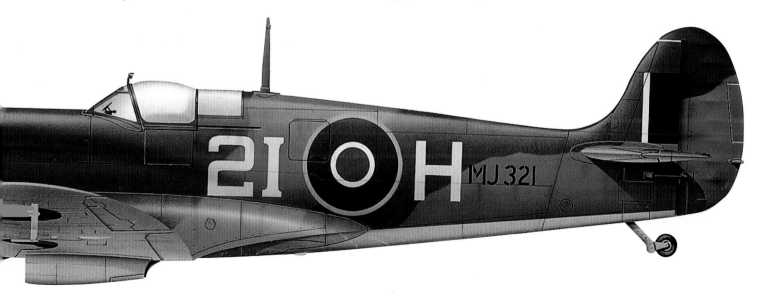

Right: Spitfire Mk II P8131 of No 276 Squadron was one of 50 converted for air-sea rescue work to drop survival equipment from flare chutes.

Below: Spitfire Mk IXC preparing for take-off on a night intruder sortie. Note the under-fuselage auxiliary tank.

damaged, the enemy aircraft breaking away after being hit by cannon fire and going down followed by Sgt Buglass, who lost sight of it. Shepherd went to Hallingworth's rescue when he was being attacked, and was himself fired at head-on by two Fw 190s. Flight Sergeant Cross is missing from this engagement; no one saw what happened to him, but as he was flying number two to Shepherd it is believed that he must have been hit during the double attack on his section leader. The Squadron got split up during the engagement, seven aircraft coming back together and the other four in two pairs. No one saw Cross crash. He was a very nice, quiet Canadian and will be very much missed.'

Deep penetration

From the spring of 1943 the fighter wings of No 11 Group equipped with the Spitfire IX were also assigned to escort duties with the US Eighth Army Air Force, which began deep-penetration missions into Germany in March. The Spitfires' limited range meant that escort could only be provided for part of the way, leaving the bombers to continue unescorted into Germany. The Luftwaffe soon shattered the illusion that large formations of heavy bombers could operate deep inside enemy territory without fighter escort, relying entirely on their defensive armament. Some of the heaviest fighting took place over Holland, a main route into Germany for the Allied bomber squadrons. By the summer of 1943 almost all the Spitfire squadrons had rearmed with the Mk IX, and for escort missions the fighters were given auxiliary fuel tanks. A 30-gallon 'slipper' type belly tank was fitted, which could be jettisoned before combat. Although unsatisfactory in many respects it served its purpose, and some 300,000 were produced for use by the Spitfire squadrons.

Repeated attacks

Pilots were content with the Spitfire Mk IX, which many considered to be superior to the Focke-Wulf 190 at medium and low level. One pilot, Squadron Leader D.G. Andrews, showed what the aircraft could do in skilled hands when faced with superior numbers. His squadron was escorting USAAF B-26 Marauders on a raid to Woensdrecht when, having turned back because of bad weather, the Spitfires were attacked by more than a dozen Fw 190s over the island of Walcheren. One Spitfire was shot down and the squadron became scattered.

Andrews was subjected to repeated attacks from ahead, abeam and astern, which damaged his Spitfire in several places and put the R/T out of action. Unable to call for help, Andrews lost height almost to ground level near Walcheren in an attempt to shake off his pursuers, though he now had to face ground fire as well. Gradually, the number of enemy aircraft decreased until only four attackers were left, although Andrews could make little homeward progress because of the need to take constant evasive action. Up to this point Andrews had had no opportunity to fire his guns, but by the time he was ten miles west of Walcheren, having shaken off another two Focke-Wulfs, he was in a position to turn against the remaining enemy fighters. This unexpected move caused one of the enemy to fly directly into Andrews' concentrated fire; the Fw 190 dived into the sea with a tremendous splash and the other immediately disengaged, leaving Andrews free to return to his base at Manston.

Frustrating time

Despite the provision of auxiliary fuel tanks, the Spitfire's limited range meant that it could only provide bomber escort to a point midway across the Netherlands. Its main usefulness therefore lay in meeting the bombers as they returned, when they were at their most vulnerable, short of ammunition

Below: Ground crew preparing a Spitfire VB of No 322 (Norwegian) Squadron for a sortie from RAF Catterick, Yorshire, in 1942.

Right: This Spitfire Mk IX, BF274, never officially existed. It carried the wrong serial number throughout its service life, for reasons that were never explained.

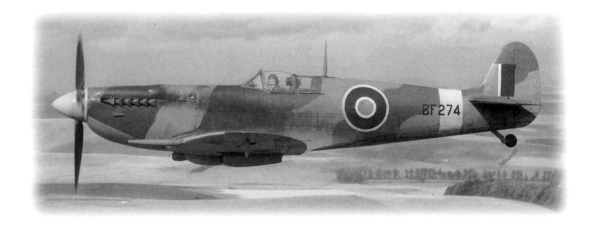

Right: This Spitfire Mk IX, BF274, never officially existed. It carried the wrong serial number throughout its service life, for reasons that were never explained.

Below: Pilots of No 340 'Ile de France' Squadron practise a scramble at Westhampnett in 1942.

and with their crews exhausted. For the Spitfire pilots it was a frustrating time.

Despite serious losses sustained in the summer of 1943, particularly during the so-called 'anniversary raids' of August, General Eaker, commanding the US VIII Bomber Command, was determined to maintain the daylight offensive. Early in October it was judged that the Eighth Air Force was ready to resume its deep-penetration attacks. But when the US bombers did so, the lessons of August were soon rammed home even more forcibly. In one week between 8 and 14 October, when the Americans attacked Bremen, Marienburg, Danzig, Münster and once again Schweinfurt, they lost 148 bombers and nearly 1500 aircrew. In the Schweinfurt raid of 14 October,

which became known as Black Thursday, the Luftwaffe flew over 500 sorties and destroyed 60 of the 280 bombers taking part – over 20 per cent.

Wing Commander J.E. 'Johnnie' Johnson, then the Kenley Wing Leader (he was to become the RAF's top-scoring Spitfire pilot with 38 victories), commanded a formation of Spitfires heading out to escort the returning bombers. He described the aftermath of this terrible encounter:

'It was a clear afternoon, and we first saw their contrails many miles away, as well as the thinner darting contrails of the enemy fighters above and on either flank. As we closed the gap we could see that they had taken a terrible mauling, for there were gaping holes in their precise formations. Some Fortresses were gradually losing height, and a few

straggglers, lagging well behind, were struggling to get home on three engines.

'We swept well behind the stragglers and drove off a few 109s and 110s, but the great air battle was over, and what a fight it must have been, because more than half the bombers we nursed across the North Sea were shot up. One or two ditched in the sea, and many others, carrying dead and badly injured crew members, had to make crash-landings. How we longed for more drop tanks, so that some of the many hundreds of Spitfires based in Britain could play their part in the great battles over Germany…'

Favourite prey

Among the hundreds of other Spitfire pilots who flew bomber escort missions was Pierre Clostermann, a French fighter ace flying with the RAF, who wrote in his book *The Big Show*:

'Behind the formation were the stragglers, making for the coast, for the haven of refuge of an advanced air base on the other side of the Channel, flying only by a sublime effort of will… You could imagine the blood pouring over the heaps of empty cartridges, the pilot nursing his remaining engines

and anxiously eyeing the long white trail of petrol escaping from his riddled tanks. These isolated Fortresses were the Focke-Wulf's favourite prey. Therefore the squadrons detached two or three pairs of Spitfires, charged with bringing each one back safe: an exhausting task as these damaged Fortresses often dragged along on a third of their total power, stretching the endurance of their escort to the limit… In many cases it was only the moral support of the presence of a pair of Spitfires that gave them the courage to hold out to the end, to resist the temptation of baling out and waiting for the end of the war in some Oflag or other.'

As the end of 1943 approached, many of the UK-based Spitfire squadrons were preparing for a different role. In June 1943 the Second Tactical Air Force was formed to provide tactical support for the 1st Canadian and 2nd British Armies in the forthcoming invasion. By June 1944, 32 Spitfire squadrons were assigned to Second TAF, while 22 more were retained in the UK for air defence. In November 1943, Fighter Command was renamed Air Defence of Great Britain; a year later there was an about-face, and it became Fighter Command again – to much rejoicing among its personnel.

Above: **A Spitfire of No 453 (Canadian) Squadron being prepared for D-Day operations on 5 June 1944. The aircraft wears black and white 'invasion' stripes.**

CHAPTER FOUR

The Griffon-engined and Photo-recce Spitfires

Another development of the Rolls-Royce 'R' engine, which had powered the Supermarine S6 racing seaplane series, was the '37', built in 1939. Named Griffon, after the mythical bird, it produced 1294kW (1735hp) and weighed 900kg (1980lb). Although it had a larger frontal area than the Merlin, fitting it to a Spitfire airframe was a logical next step.

Opposite: The Battle of Britain Memorial Flight Spitfire Mk XIX, the last of the PR Spitfires, in D-Day recognition stripes.

Below: The underside of a Spitfire was not a particularly pretty sight. Seen here is a Mk XII, the first of the Griffon-engined Spitfires.

The Griffon was under development for naval aircraft, and it was the IIB version that first became available for installation in a Spitfire. The airframe selected was that of the Spitfire Mk IV prototype, DP845 (not to be confused with the PR IV, which was unconnected). Trials proved satisfactory and an order for 750 Mk IVs was placed, but this was later cancelled and it was not until 1942 that 100 Spitfires, designated Mk XIIs, were converted to Griffon engines.

These aircraft had been either Mk Vs in the process of being converted to Mk IX standard, or Mk VIIIs which were still on the production line. The Mk XII was given extra length and the fuselage was strengthened to compensate for the extra weight and power of the Griffon. As a result of its greater frontal area, the engine cowling had to be given two pronounced bulges to cover the cylinder banks. The propeller was a four-blade Rotol. The Griffon propeller shaft rotated in the opposite direction to that of the Merlin, and this produced a strong swing to the right on take-off. About half of the Mk XIIs produced had retractable tailwheels, depending on whether the individual aircraft was converted from a Mk V/IX or Mk VIII airframe. The Mk XII had clipped wings, as it was intended for use only as a low-level interceptor. Armament was two cannon and four machine guns, like that of the Mk VIII and

Mk IX. Maximum cruising speed was a fast 585km/h (364mph), but this gave a short range of only 529km (329 miles). The Mk XII could reach 1500m (5000ft) in a little over a minute after take-off, but it needed 6.7 minutes to reach 6100m (20,000ft). Maximum speed at 1680m (5500ft) was 598km/h (372mph), rising to 632km/h (393mph) at 5490m (18,000ft).

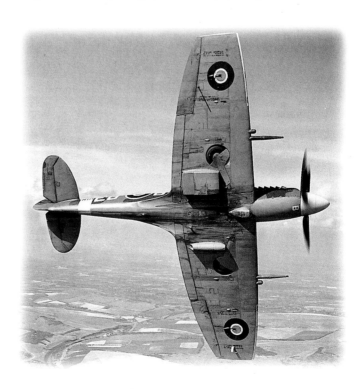

Low-level attacks

The Mk XII was developed specifically to counter low-level attacks on the English south coast by German fighter-bombers, which were becoming increasingly troublesome in the first half of 1942.

The principal Luftwaffe units involved in attacks on the south coast at this time were Jagdgeschwader 2 and 26. Armed with the Messerschmitt Bf 109F-4/B fitted with racks for a 250kg (550lb) bomb, they specialized in low-level intruder operations. Often taking off in poor visibility from their well-defended airfields at Abbeville, Ligescourt, Poix or St Omer, they would hug the ground and head out over the Channel at wave-top height. Favourite targets were the towns of Dover, Brighton, Folkestone, Worthing and Newhaven. JG2 (based to the south around Evreux and Caen) concentrated its attacks on Channel shipping, while JG26 attacked the coastal towns.

Pure luck

This type of attack was hurried and literally hit-or-miss, but it kept the RAF's fighter defences in a state of constant alert. Once the fighter-bombers had made their attack, defending Spitfires stood little chance of catching them on the homeward run, and it was a matter of pure luck if a patrol intercepted them on the way in. The situation became even worse from June 1942, when the

fighter-bomber Geschwader on the Channel coast began to rearm with the Focke-Wulf Fw 190A-3, which could carry a 500kg (1100lb) bomb. Enemy attacks, usually carried out by a Schwarm of four aircraft, reached new levels of success, and it was fortunate for the British that JG2 and 26 never had more than about 20 Fw 190s available for operations at any one time. In an attempt to redress the situation the RAF's latest fighter, the Hawker Typhoon, was rushed into action; but the Typhoon was suffering from a series of development problems, and so the deployment of the Spitfire XII was accelerated.

Daylight raid

On 20 January 1943 the third Spitfire XII, EN223, flew to Manston in Kent from the Air Fighting Development Unit at Duxford, where it had been undergoing trials. At this time the Typhoons of No 609 Squadron were based at Manston, and the lone Spitfire's arrival coincided with a daylight raid on London by 28 Fw 190s and Bf 109s. The Manston fighters were scrambled in time to intercept the raiders as they left the target area and they destroyed four Fw 190s and three Bf 109s, one of the Focke-Wulfs being shot down by Squadron Leader R.H. Harris of No 91 Squadron, flying the Spitfire XII.

The first squadron to equip fully with the Spitfire XII, in February 1943, was No 41

Below: **Bomb-carrying Spitfire XII HB878 of No 41 Squadron, one of three units to be equipped with the type.**

Spitfire Mk XIVE

SPITFIRE MK XIVE

Type: single-seat fighter-bomber

Powerplant: one Rolls-Royce Griffon 65 or 66 Vee-12 piston engine rated at 1517kW (2035hp) at altitude

Performance: maximum speed 721km/h (448mph) at 7925m (26,000ft); range with internal fuel 740km (460 miles); service ceiling 13,100km (43,000ft)

Dimensions: span 11.23m (36ft 10in); length 9.96m (32ft 8in); height 3.87m (12ft 8in); wing area 22.67m² (244 sq ft)

Squadron, which shot down its first FW 190 on 27 April, while operating from Hawkinge. The second unit to re-equip with the Mk XII, No 91, destroyed five enemy fighter-bombers in a running battle over the Channel on 25 May 1943. In June 1943, following a marked decline in enemy fighter-bomber activity, and with the Typhoons now well able to cope with the situation, the two Spitfire XII-equipped squadrons moved to Westhampnett to form a bomber support wing.

Right: Fine study of a Spitfire XII. The type was rushed into service to counter enemy fighter-bombers intruding at low level.

Right: Supermarine Spitfire LF.Mk XVI SL721. The aircraft was used as the personal transport of Air Marshal Sir James Robb, AOC-in-C RAF Fighter Command, 1945–47.

No 41 Squadron shepherded 60 B-17s home from Le Mans on 26 June, and with the arrival of No 91 Squadron a couple of days later the Wing began escorting the medium bombers of No 2 Group and also Typhoon fighter-bombers. Nos 41 and 91 Squadrons were the only operational units to be armed with the Spitfire XII, although a few examples were used by No 595 Squadron for anti-aircraft co-operation duties at Aberporth, Wales, from December 1944 to July 1945.

Large-scale production

The next Griffon-engined Spitfire variant was Mk XIV. Based on a Mk VIII airframe, it was the first Griffon-engined Spitfire variant to go into large-scale production, a total of 957 being built. The first aircraft were issued to No 322 (Netherlands) and No 610 Squadrons in March and April 1944. The Mk XIV's most distinctive feature was a five-blade Rotol propeller, driven by a 1517kW (2035hp) Griffon 65. The Mk XIV had a maximum speed of 720km/h

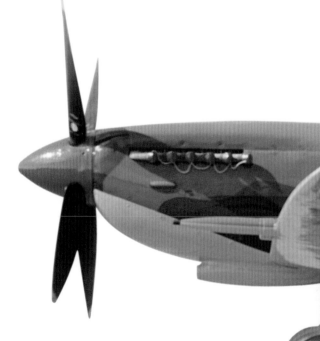

(448mph) at 7930m (26,000ft) and 670km/h (417mph) at 3660m (12,000 ft), which made it a very fast aircraft indeed. Together with the Spitfire XII, it was pressed into service to combat the V-1 flying bombs, the first of which fell on British soil on 12 June 1944.

The Mks XII and XIV both performed well against the V-1. 14 pilots of No 91 Squadron flying the Mk XII destroyed five or more flying bombs apiece, and five pilots had scores of over ten. Both 41 and 91 Squadrons exchanged their Mk XIIs for Mk XIVs before the V-1 offensive was over. Spitfire squadrons also carried out many dive-bombing attacks on V-1 launching sites in the Pas de Calais; these continued until September 1944, when the sites were overrun. The Spitfire XIV's speed also gave it a good chance of catching Me 262 jet fighters, several of which were destroyed by the Spitfires of No 127 Wing based in Belgium in the latter part of 1944 and in 1945.

Final development

The Spitfire Mk XVIII was the last Griffon-engined development of the original Spitfire airframe and was almost identical in appearance to the Mk XIV, except that the latter's 'universal' Spitfire wing was replaced by a specially designed one. The first 100

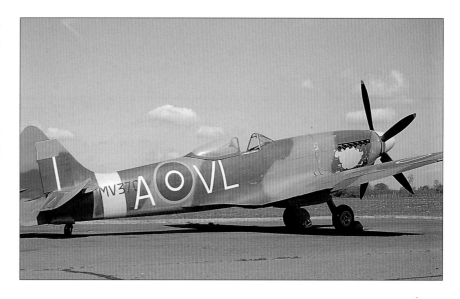

aircraft were completed as fighters, and a further 200 as FR.XVIII fighter-reconnaissance aircraft. Production aircraft were not available before the middle of 1945 and so the type did not see operational service in WWII, although a few examples reached the Far East before the end of hostilities. But the FR.XVIII did see action in Malaya against communist insurgents in 1948, while operating with No 81 Squadron. The type also equipped Nos 11, 28, 32, 60 and 208 Squadrons, all serving in the Middle and Far East.

Above: **Spitfire Mk XIV of No 322 (Netherlands) Squadron, which was formed at Woodvale in June 1943 and which operated Spitfires until October 1945.**

Above: Spitfire F XIV RB140 seen here in its early form. The first six aircraft were converted from Mk VIII airframes at Rolls-Royce's Hucknall factory.

New wing

The next Griffon Spitfire was the F.21, which represented a major redesign of the Spitfire airframe. In fact, the F.21 bore so little resemblance to the original Spitfire that at one point the name Victor was mooted for it. Although thousands were on order before the end of WWII, only 120 examples were actually produced. The F.21 had a new, strengthened wing, with provision for four cannon. The day of the airborne machine gun was over, in the RAF at least. An increase in weight made it necessary to reposition the undercarriage, which when retracted was fully enclosed by wheel flaps. The tail wheel was also retractable and the aircraft had a new, broad-chord vertical tail unit. Metal-covered elevators and rudder and 86kg (190lb) of armour plating contributed to an empty weight of 3244kg (7160lb), making this the heaviest Spitfire so far.

The F.21 was nevertheless a handsome aircraft,

and entered service at the end of 1945. Powered by the Griffon 61, the F.21's maximum speed was 724km (450mph) at heights from 5795m (19,000ft) to 7930m (26,000ft), 676km/h (420mph) at 3660m (12,000ft) and 627km/h (390mph) at sea level. Its internal fuel capacity of 120 gallons gave it a range of 788km (490 miles) at 458km/h (285mph), the range being boosted to 1415km (880 miles) with maximum auxiliary fuel. The Spitfire 21 equipped eight squadrons, three of them Auxiliary Air Force units.

Another Spitfire variant, the F.22, came off the production line at the same time as the F.21. Apart from a cut-down fuselage, a revised

---

SPITFIRE PR.MK XIX

Type: single-seat reconnaissance aircraft

Powerplant: one Rolls-Royce Griffon 65 Vee-12 piston engine rated at 1528kW (2050hp) at altitude

Performance: maximum speed 721km/h (448mph) at 7472m (24,500ft); maximum range l 745km (1085 miles); service ceiling 13,565m (44,500ft)

Dimensions: span 11.23m (36ft 10in); length 9.96m (32ft 8in); height 3.87m (12ft 8in); wing area 22.67m² (244 sq ft)

Left: The Spitfire XIV prototype, JF318, was converted from a Mk VIII airframe. It was a more powerful fighter at all altitudes than the low-level Mk XII.

cockpit canopy and a 24-volt electrical system instead of the F.21's 12-volt, there were no differences between the two. Production of the F.22 began in March 1945 and 260 were built, the original order for 627 having been reduced. The Spitfire F.22 equipped 13 squadrons, all but one being Auxiliary units. The exception was No 73 Squadron, which used its F.22s at Ta' Qali, Malta, until 1948.

Last Spitfire

Spitfire PR.Mk XIX

The last of the long line of Spitfires, and according to some the most beautiful of them all, was the F.24. Only 81 F.24s were produced, which were in effect modified F.22s. The only squadron to be armed with the type was No 80, at Kai Tak, Hong Kong; this unit maintained a high state of alert during the Chinese Civil War and also during the early months of the Korean War. Occasionally, its aircraft made fast incursions into Chinese air space to monitor airfields and military installations.

On Battle of Britain Sunday, 1951, before handing over its aircraft to the Hong Kong Auxiliary Air Force, No 80 Squadron carried out a

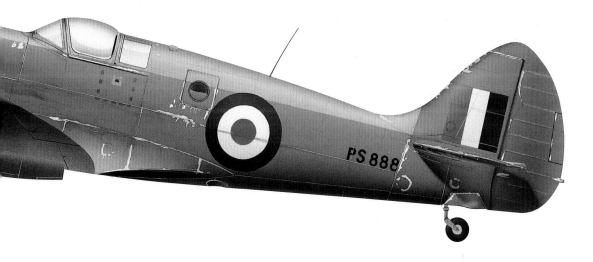

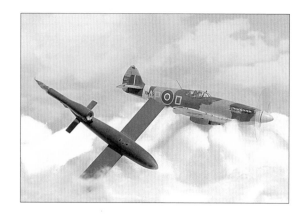

memorial flypast. It was the last time that a Spitfire squadron performed this tribute.

Photo-reconnaissance

The Spitfire performed the vital task of photographic reconnaissance throughout World War II. The first two aircraft – Spitfire Is N3069 and N3071 – were delivered to Heston, Middlesex, where the RAF's embryo PR organization was based, on 13 October 1939. In November, stripped of all non-essential equipment and fitted with an F.24 camera, the second of these aircraft deployed to Seclin near Lille, and on the 18th of that month it

carried out the first Spitfire PR flight, over Aachen. The Spitfire's limited range was a problem, but the provision of extra fuel tanks extended this to around 1200km (750 miles). The modified aircraft were designated Spitfire PR.IB.

In January 1940 the PR organization at Heston was renamed the Photographic Development Unit (PDU), and the Special Survey Flight (the cover name for the unit responsible for clandestine reconnaissance flights before the war) became No 212 (PR) Squadron. By spring 1940 the Spitfires had photographed almost the entire Ruhr and, together with the PR Blenheims also used by the squadron, had located all the major surface vessels of the German fleet. In July 1940 the PDU was designated No 1 Photographic Reconnaissance Unit (PRU).

Zeiss camera

The next PRU to be formed, on 16 November 1940, was No 3 at RAF Oakington near Cambridge. It had an initial establishment of six Spitfires and two Wellingtons. The first Spitfire sortie, to Cologne, was flown on 29 November. Ironically the aircraft was fitted with a Zeiss

Left: Spitfire XIV of No 350 (Belgian) Squadron. The first Belgian-manned RAF fighter squadron, No 350, was formed at Valley, Anglesey, in November 1941.

Below: Spitfire LF.XVI bearing the code letters of the Central Gunnery School. Flying Training Command units carried four-letter identity codes in 1946.

camera taken from a Junkers Ju 88 of a Luftwaffe reconnaissance unit, 4(F)121, forced down at Oakington with engine trouble on 19 September. No 2 PRU, formed in June 1941, was based at Heliopolis, Egypt, but did not receive Spitfires until 1942, having been equipped until then with Hurricanes and a Lockheed Model 12A. The Spitfires were PR Mk IVs, which were converted Mk Vs. The conversion involved sealing the wing torsion box forward of the main spar to form integral fuel and oil tanks. No armament was fitted and instead 300-litre (66-gallon) fuel tanks were incorporated, giving the aircraft sufficient radius of action to take it as far as Greece. The

Above: Spitfire F.21 of the Central Fighter Establishment. The F.21 was used in a wide variety of training roles in the post-war years.

total fuel capacity was 977 litres (215 gallons), giving a range of 2250–2400km (1400–1500 miles). No 4 PRU was formed to provide photographic intelligence before and during the Allied landings in North Africa in November 1942 and subsequently operated from Maison Blanche, Algeria.

Armed version

The Spitfire PR.VII, which was also a Mk IV conversion, was basically an armed version of the PR.IV, having an 'A' type armament of eight machine guns and an extra fuel tank only in the rear fuselage. Inevitably, it was not long before the superior high-altitude performance of the Spitfire Mk IX, with its Merlin 61 engine, led to the development of a

Right: Head-on view of the Spitfire F.22, a variant that equipped many Auxiliary Air Force units in the years after the war, before jet equipment arrived.

photographic reconnaissance version, the PR.XI. Paradoxically, the aircraft that was developed from the PR.XI, and followed it, was designated Mk X; it featured a pressurized cockpit and was not a success, only 16 aircraft being produced. These were used from July 1944 to April 1945 by No 542 Squadron, based at Benson in Oxfordshire.

The PR.XIII was designed for low-level work; 18 Mk V airframes were converted and fitted with the Merlin 32 engine. The PR.XIII was the last of the Merlin-engined Spitfires, being followed by the Griffon-engined PR.XIX. Basically, the latter was a late production Mk XIV airframe fitted with a bowser wing (a wing adapted as a fuel tank), with a universal camera installation based on that of the PR.IV/XI. It was developed early in 1944 to give greater range, speed and ceiling than existing PR Spitfires, both to elude the German defences, whose methods of detection and interception had steadily improved, and to meet the requirements of operations in the Far East.

The first of 225 Mk.XIXs was delivered in May 1944. It was intended that the type would be replaced on the production line by a PR version of the Spiteful, but prolonged delays in the development of this aircraft ultimately led to its cancellation. Due to the increased weight of the Griffon, together with petrol-filled wing leading edges, the PR.XIX was more nose-heavy than any other Spitfire type, and particular care had to be exercised when taxiing before take-off. The PR.XIX remained in service in the Far East until 1954, performing valuable photographic work with No 81 Squadron during the Malayan Emergency, and was used for meteorological tasks until 1957.

Substantial size

By the end of 1943 ten specialist PR squadrons, seven of them equipped with Spitfires, had been formed at home and overseas within the framework of the PRUs, which had now grown to a substantial size. The first Spitfire PR squadrons were Nos 541 and 542, formed respectively from B and F, and A and E Flights of No 1 PRU at Benson. A third squadron, No 543, also formed at Benson in October 1943. Overseas, No 680 Squadron formed at Matariya in North Africa on 1 February 1943, and on the same day No 682 Squadron

formed at Maison Blanche from No 4 PRU. On 8 February 1943 No 683 Squadron formed from B Flight of No 69 Squadron at Luqa, Malta. In the meantime, No 3 PRU had deployed to the Far East, where No 681 Squadron was formed from it in January 1943 at Dum Dum, Calcutta. Also in 1943, No 106 Group was established at Benson to control all RAF PR training, operations and photographic interpretation.

This expansion meant that PR Spitfires operated in all theatres, from Burma to the Arctic. In August 1942, following the destruction of the Russia-bound convoy PQ17, three Spitfire PR.IVs of No 1 PRU deployed to Vayenga, North Russia, to

Below: A Spitfire Mk 22 displaying its graceful lines. The laminar-flow wing surface is marred only by the blisters over the four cannon.

keep watch on enemy surface raiders. The Spitfires carried Soviet markings and the first operation was flown over Altenfjord, Norway, on 10 September. The detachment returned to the UK in November and a second one went to Vaenga in April 1943. This maintained surveillance on the *Tirpitz*, and as a result of the PR activity the German battleship was badly damaged when she was attacked in her anchorage by midget submarines on 22 September.

Above: Apart from some equipment changes, there was no difference between the Spitfire F.22 and the F.24, seen here. F.24s served in Hong Kong into the 1950s.

It was a PR Spitfire, too, that located *Tirpitz*'s sister ship, *Bismarck*, heading for the North Atlantic via a Norwegian fjord in May 1941, beginning a pursuit that ended with the battleship's destruction several days later.

Perils

In North Africa, the commanding officer of No 4 PRU was Wing Commander (later Air Marshal Sir) Alfred Ball, who later provided an interesting insight into the perils faced by a PR pilot:

'In Tunisia at the end of '42 we had a lot of large area photography to do, mostly front-line mapping for First Army. It was very costly and on one occasion we lost four aircraft in three days from a squadron of nine. The difficulty was the great concentration of Fw 190s and Me 109Gs and standing patrols in the battle area (our own fighters were having a bad time just then, December '42 and January '43). In this case the problem was solved by the replacement of our Mk IV Spitfires by Mk XIs while our fighter squadrons got Mk IXs.

Left: Spitfire F.22 PK312, with F.21 LA232 behind, poses for the camera of renowned aviation photographer Charles E. Brown.

'Let me outline an experience in a Spitfire Mk IV at 24,000 feet (a bad height for the Spitfire but ideal for the Fw 190) near Tunis. I was just completing some 45 minutes of front line photography when I spotted four Fw 190s some three to four miles away and about 1000 feet below going in the opposite direction. They turned to me shortly after I saw them and I opened up to full throttle and dived slightly to gain speed as quickly as possible. Within a very few minutes, however, they were on to me and the first of eight attacks took place. My only chance lay in out-turning them. In the event I was hit by the very first burst of fire – having left my turn (maximum possible)

Below: Spitfire F.22 of No 602 'City of Glasgow' Squadron, Royal Auxiliary Air Force, pictured at Abbotsinch in 1948. The squadron used F.22s until 1951.

a fraction too late – but although the aircraft was hit in a number of interesting places, the damage was not catastrophic. This one-sided combat went on for five to ten minutes until the Focke-Wulfs broke off, either out of ammunition or short of fuel.'

Early sighting

'I have touched on interception risks but not on the capabilities of PR Spitfires and enemy fighters – Me 109Es and Fs until mid-1942, then increasingly Gs and Fw 190s. Until the end of 1942 we were still flying the old Mk IVs with Merlin 45 engines. We could match the Es in speed and cope with the Fs too, provided we saw them in time, for we could out-turn them, but we

Above: Spitfire PR.IV BR416 spent most of its operational career based in Palestine. The PR.IV was the first variant to adopt the Type D wing, all armament being replaced by extra fuel.

Right: Last of the Spitfires. In this superb shot, a Spitfire F.24 is flanked by a Mk 21 and Mk.22. Compare the wing shape with that of earlier Spitfires.

could not afford to lose much height as they could always outdive us. It was another story with the 109Gs and 190s. They were both faster, but the 190's best height was around 24,000 feet and provided we could stay at 30,000 feet, we had a chance at full throttle, but it depended on an early sighting of the enemy fighters, and preferably well before they saw you. The 109G had a better ceiling than the 190 but we could out-turn them both, so an experienced pilot could get away with it so long as he got his time to turn just right, but it was touch and go until we received the Spitfire Mk XI in early 1943.'

As a result of these developments, the PR loss rate, which was just about acceptable during the first two years of the war, became quite serious in the last six months of '42 and in early '43, particularly over north-west Germany, where experienced pilots only were allowed to operate, and in Tunisia, where there was that unusual concentration of 190s and 109Gs covering Rommel's last stand against Montgomery in North Africa. For the remainder of the war, however, Mk XI (Merlin 60 Series engine) and, later, Mk XIX (Griffon engine) Spitfires were able to range freely over Germany, and indeed worldwide, with acceptable losses, even when they came up against the jet-engined Me 262 and the Me 163 rocket-powered fighter.

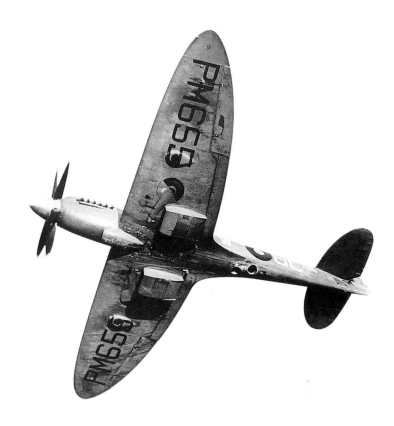

It is for its contribution to the RAF's victory in the Battle of Britain that the Spitfire is best remembered. But the contribution made by a relatively small number of PR Spitfires to the overall Allied victory was truly outstanding.

Above: **Supermarine Spitfire PR.XIX PM665 of the Central Photographic Development Unit, which continued to operate this mark into the early 1950s.**

Left: **Spitfire PR.XIX pictured early in 1945, fitted with a long-range fuel tank. The PR.XIX was intended to cope with more advanced enemy air defences.**

Left: Spitfire PR.XIX PS915 of the BBMF flying over Warton, Samlesbury and Fylde on 19 March 1987. It was delivered to the RAF in April 1945.

CHAPTER FIVE

Spitfires Abroad

From 11 June 1940, the day after Italy declared war on the Allies, the strategically vital island of Malta came under almost constant air attack. The initial attacks on the island by the Regia Aeronautica were opposed at first by a trio of Gloster Sea Gladiators and a handful of Hurricanes, and it was the latter aircraft that bore the brunt of the enemy onslaught for 18 months – until the first Spitfires arrived.

On 7 March 1942, in an operation code-named Spotter, 15 Spitfires flew off the aircraft carriers *Eagle* and *Argus* at extreme range. All the aircraft arrived safely in Malta, as did nine more on 21 March (Operation Picket I) and seven more on 29 March (Operation Picket II). The newcomers were divided among the three Hurricane squadrons defending the island, Nos 126, 185 and 249 (which had only 30 serviceable aircraft between them). The arrival of the Spitfires enabled the air defences to hold out for another month or so, but after that the position once again became desperate.

On 20 April 1942 Operation Calendar was mounted, in which 47 more Spitfires reached the island after flying from the aircraft carrier USS *Wasp*. But their arrival had been detected by the Germans, and within hours the airfields were under attack. By the end of the next day, after further heavy raids, only 18 of the original 47 Spitfires were still airworthy. For the first time, Operation Calendar involved the deployment of a complete Spitfire squadron to Malta; this was No 603, transferred to the island from its base at Peterhead in Scotland. 603 had been one of the first Spitfire squadrons to engage the Luftwaffe, right at the start of the war.

Climax of the raids

On 9 May the USS *Wasp* returned with HMS *Eagle*, and between them the carriers flew off 64 more Spitfires, which went into action almost immediately. The following day saw a major air battle over the island when the Lufwaffe made a determined effort to sink the minelayer HMS *Welshman*, which had docked in Valletta harbour laden with supplies and ammunition. Between them the island's Spitfires and

Opposite: A Spitfire Mk VA (Trop) pictured against a background of palm trees in Tunisia in 1943. The Mk V was the 'workhorse' Spitfire.

Below: A Spitfire Mk VB, equipped with long-range tank, about to leave the aircraft carrier USS *Wasp* for Malta on 9 May 1942.

Above: Seafire III of No 807 Squadron comes to grief on the escort carrier HMS *Hunter*. A great many Seafires were written off in accidents of this kind.

Hurricanes flew 124 sorties that day, destroying 15 enemy aircraft. Three Spitfires were lost, but two of the pilots survived. Seventeen more Spitfires arrived later in May and deliveries of fighter aircraft continued throughout the summer months of 1942. HMS *Eagle* alone delivered 182 Spitfires before she was sunk by a U-boat on 11 July. Most of the ferry work was undertaken by HMS *Furious*, which flew off 37 Spitfires on the day HMS *Eagle* went down,

followed by 27 more on 7 August. Several RAF pilots distinguished themselves in the summer of 1942 – one of them was Canadian-born Pilot Officer George F. Buerling, who scored 27 victories while flying Spitfires over the island. He survived the war only to be killed while ferrying an aircraft to Israel in 1948.

Last reinforcement

The last Spitfire reinforcement to Malta, Operation Train, took place on 25 October when HMS *Furious* flew off 31 aircraft, of which 29 reached the island. The enemy raids continued, reaching their climax in November 1942, when the Germans subjected Malta to a furious round-the-clock bombardment that lasted ten days. The defenders remained unbroken, and the offensive against the supply convoys ferrying desperately needed supplies and reinforcements to the German and Italian forces in North Africa went on almost unchecked. The battle for Malta was over; by the end of the year most of the Luftwaffe units in Sicily had been withdrawn for service on other fronts. In the early months of 1943 Malta was turned into a major supply base as the Allies built up their resources for the offensive that would take them across the narrow straits to Sicily

Below: Spitfires of No 601 Squadron, Tunisia, in company with AB502, the personal aircraft of Air Cdre Gleed, OC 224 Wing, who was shot down and killed by a Bf 109 on 16 April 1943.

and, ultimately, the Italian mainland. It was in Malta that the Spitfire was first used as a fighter-bomber, attacking enemy airfields on Sicily. It was a role that Reginald Mitchell had never envisaged for it, but one in which it was to prove very successful.

Desert Spitfires

The first Desert Air Force Spitfire squadron to become operational in North Africa was No 145, which embarked for the Middle East in February 1942 and set up at Heliopolis in Egypt in April. The following month it equipped with Spitfire Mk VBs fitted with Vokes tropical filters and moved up to Gambut, from where it flew its first mission, an escort for Hurricane fighter-bombers, on 1 June. In the next few weeks No 145 was joined by two more Spitfire squadrons deployed from the United Kingdom, Nos 92 and 601, which formed No 244 Wing of No 211 Group together with the Hurricanes of No 73 Squadron.

One of the most important benefits of the Spitfire's arrival in North Africa was that it seriously disrupted the enemy's air reconnaissance activities over the Canal Zone, which was being constantly monitored by high-flying Ju 86Ps operating from Crete. Flying at altitudes of up to 12,800m (42,000ft), these aircraft went unchallenged until personnel at the Aboukir Aircraft Depot modified a pair of Spitfires to deal with them. Two Spitfire VCs were stripped of all non-essential equipment, including armour plating. New four-bladed Rotol propellers were fitted, and the Spitfires' Merlin 46 engines were tuned to produce more power at high altitude. The usual armament of two 20mm cannon and four 7.7mm (0.303in) machine guns was also removed and replaced by two 12.7mm (0.50in) machine guns. Within a month, in August-September 1942, the modified Spitfires destroyed three Ju 86Ps, bringing an abrupt halt to overflights of the Canal Zone.

Spitfires at sea

It was in the North African theatre that the Spitfire's naval version, the Seafire, made its combat debut. Between the two world wars the Royal Navy's carrier-borne aircraft evolved at a much slower pace than their land-based counterparts. With the outbreak of WWII the RN found a partial solution to the problem of its outdated fighters by adapting land-based aircraft like the Hawker Hurricane for carrier operations, and in late 1941 it was decided to adapt the Spitfire in similar fashion under the name of Seafire. The main variants were the Seafire Mk IB (166 conversions from Spitfire VB airframes); Mk IIC (372 aircraft intended for low- and medium-altitude air combat and air reconnaissance); 30 Mk III (Hybrid) aircraft with fixed wings, followed by 1220 examples of the definitive Seafire Mk III with folding wings; and the Seafire Mks XV, XVII, 45, 46 and 47, these being Griffon-engined variants.

The Seafire saw much action in the Mediterranean in the summer of 1943 and in the Pacific in 1945. The Seafire 47, operating from HMS *Triumph*, took part in air strikes against terrorists in Malaya and against North Korean forces in the early

Below: Cactus palms and Spitfires; local people lend a hand as RAF ground crew service their aircraft at a forward operating base in Tunisia, 1943.

weeks of the Korean War. Although far from ideal for carrier operations because of its narrow-track undercarriage and long nose, the Seafire performed well and was used by RN Reserve Air Squadrons until 1954. In November 1942, two Seafire squadrons, Nos 801 and 807, provided air cover for the Allied landings in North Africa (Operation Torch), and on 8 November Lt G.C. Baldwin of No 801 Squadron scored the Seafire's first kill, shooting down a Vichy French Dewoitine D520.

American Spitfires

Spitfires also took part in Operation Torch, Nos 72, 81, 93, 111, 152 and 242 Squadrons deploying to the newly-captured Algerian airfield of Maison Blanche. In addition the USAAF's 31st Fighter Group, equipped with Spitfire VBs and operating from Gibraltar, provided air cover for US ground forces approaching the airfield of Tafaraoui, Oran. Armed with Spitfires since its arrival in England in May 1942, and originally assigned to the Eighth Air Force, the 31st FG had seen action over Dieppe in August. Now assigned to the Twelfth Air Force, it operated Spitfires until April 1944, when it re-equipped with P-51 Mustangs.

In December 1942 some Spitfire IXs were deployed to North Africa to counter the threat posed by the Fw 190, which had made its appearance in the theatre. Attached to No 145 Squadron, these aircraft were flown by a highly experienced group of Polish fighter pilots led by Squadron Leader Styanislaw Skalski and collectively known as the Polish Fighting Team, or more popularly as 'Skalski's Circus'. During an eight-week period in January and February 1943, they destroyed more enemy aircraft than any other Polish unit in the whole of that year, and the pilots were subsequently offered appointments as commanding officers of other RAF fighter squadrons. Skalski, who shot down two Bf 109s and a Ju 88 over Tunisia, became the first Pole to command an RAF fighter squadron, No 601. In 1944 he was promoted to Wing Commander and led No 2 (Polish) Wing for the rest of his career, flying Mustangs. He ended the war with a score of 19 enemy aircraft destroyed, four of them over his native Poland in 1939.

Slaughtered

In February 1943 enough Spitfire IXs had arrived in North Africa to equip No 72 Squadron, just in

Right: **A Seafire Mk XV, showing the folding wing arrangement. The Seafire XV was the first Griffon-engined example of the naval fighter.**

Right: These Spitfire VBs, seen at the Persian Gulf port of Abadan in April 1943, are undergoing a pre-delivery inspection prior to being handed over to the USSR.

time for the Allied offensive that would end on 7 April with the link-up of the US II Corps and the British Eighth Army in Tunisia. At the same time the Allied air forces launched a series of heavy attacks on enemy airfields on Sicily and in southern Italy, where fleets of transport aircraft were being assembled for a desperate, last-ditch effort to send reinforcements and supplies to the

crumbling and demoralized Afrika Korps.

The Junkers Ju 52 and Messerschmitt 323 transport aircraft that survived the airfield attacks and attempted to fly to the German-held airfields in Tunisia were caught by formations of Allied fighters, often while still far out to sea, and slaughtered. On 18 April 1943, for example, 47 P-40 Warhawks of the US Ninth Air Force, together with 12 Spitfires of No 92 Squadron RAF, intercepted a formation of 90 Ju 52s escorted by 50 German and Italian fighters and destroyed 77 of them for the loss of six Warhawks and a Spitfire. This great air battle, called the Palm Sunday Massacre, resulted in the destruction of more enemy aircraft than the RAF shot down in one day at the height of the Battle of

Below: A Seafire XV hooks the wire on the escort carrier HMS *Pretoria Castle* in August 1945, at the very end of the Pacific war.

Britain. On 22 April RAF Spitfires followed up this success by shooting down 21 massive Me 323 six-engined transports, all heavily laden with troops. It was the end. On 13 May 1943 the remnants of the Afrika Korps finally surrendered.

Sicily

Having had their first taste of action in Operation Torch in November 1942, the Fleet Air Arm's Seafires featured prominently in the Allied invasion of Sicily on 9 July 1943. Aircraft of Nos 807, 880, 885 and 899 Squadrons operated from the fleet carriers *Formidable* and *Indomitable* to provide air cover over the beachheads. On 13 July the Spitfire squadrons of No 244 Wing deployed to the Sicilian airfield of Pachino from Malta, and on the same day the Spitfires of the USAAF's 31st Fighter Group flew into Agrigento. The arrival of more Spitfire units in the days that followed ensured full air support for the Allied ground forces in their conquest of the island.

On 3 September British forces landed at

Reggio di Calabria on the Italian mainland, and on the 9th a second Allied landing was made at Salerno. Combat air patrols were flown by Seafires, operating from five escort carriers; 60 Seafires were lost in five days, the majority in landing accidents. On the credit side, only two enemy fighter-bombers were shot down and four damaged, a poor result attributed to the fact that the Seafire was not fast enough to catch the Messerschmitt 109F. The surviving Seafires were deployed to an airstrip at Paestum, where they were joined by the Spitfires of No 324 Wing. In the months that followed the Spitfire squadrons flew many ground attack sorties against pinpoint targets in Italy like railway and road bridges with considerable success, alternating these operations with bomber escort. On 30 January 1944, the Spitfires of No 7 Wing South African Air Force, which had crossed the Apennines to support the US Fifth Army's offensive, escorted 215 B-17s and B-24s in an attack on four enemy airfields. The bombers dropped 29,000 fragmentation bombs,

Below: **Seafires ranged on the deck of a Royal Navy carrier, about to take off for Sicily in support of the Allied landings of July 1943.**

Left: Spitfire VCs of No 43 Squadron at Comiso airfield, Sicily, after the island was captured in July 1943. ES352 was stricken in April 1944.

causing much damage among enemy fighters assembling to intercept American bombers operating from Foggia against targets in Austria and southern Germany.

German fighters put in only occasional appearances during this period, but they were frequent enough to make bomber escort a necessity, and there were a number of combats. On 24 April 1944, for example, No 451 Squadron RAAF, which had arrived at Poretta in Corsica with its Spitfire Vs a week earlier, was escorting 25 B-25 Mitchell medium bombers in an attack on Orvieto when it was engaged by ten Fw 190s and four Bf 109s. No Spitfires were lost and the Germans were beaten off, although no claims were made by the Australians. On 25 May, No 451 Squadron destroyed three Fw 190s near Roccalbegna.

Balkan Air Force

The three Spitfire squadrons of No 7 Wing SAAF plus that of No 451 Squadron RAAF were assigned to Operation Dragoon, the Allied invasion of

Below: Spitfire Mk VIII JF880 of No 417 (City of Windsor) Squadron, RCAF, at Fano, Italy, on 29 December 1944.

Above: Spitfire IXs of No 241 Squadron against the majestic backdrop of Mount Vesuvius in the spring of 1944.

operate from Italian airfields, sending detachments to the Adriatic island of Vis in order to fly fighter sweeps over Yugoslavia. In April 1945 both squadrons moved to the captured airfield of Prkos, in Yugoslavia itself.

In the summer of 1944 some of the Spitfire squadrons in Italy rearmed with the Mk IX, and 53 Mk Vs were released for service with the Italian Co-Belligerent Air Force, which was fighting on the side of the Allies. The Spitfires were somewhat war-weary and only 33 could be made serviceable, serving with the Gruppo 20 of Stormo 51 alongside the unit's Macchi C202s and C205s. The Italian Spitfires flew their last mission of World War II on 5 May 1945, when two aircraft made a reconnaissance of the Zagreb area.

Spitfires against the Japanese

On 19 February 1942 the Japanese 1st Carrier Air Fleet launched a heavy attack on the North Australian harbour of Port Darwin. Attacks on Darwin and other strategic targets in northern Australia continued throughout the year, and were opposed by P-39s and P-40s, neither of which was a match for the Mitsubishi Zero fighter. At the request of the Australian government two UK-based RAAF Spitfire squadrons, Nos 452 and 457, were disbanded to re-form in Australia as a Spitfire Wing, together with No 54 Squadron RAF. The personnel were in place

southern France, which took place in August 1944. Other Spitfire squadrons involved in this operation were Nos 237, 238 and 253, all former Hurricane units. Several Spitfire squadrons were also included in the Balkan Air Force, created to support partisan operations in Yugoslavia and Greece; among them were Nos 335 and 336 (Hellenic) and 351 and 352 (Yugoslav) Squadrons, all formed previously in North Africa. In November 1944 the two Greek Spitfire squadrons moved to Greece, while the Yugoslav squadrons continued to

Right: Spitfire IXB of No 242 Squadron taxiing on a Corsican airstrip between March and August 1944.

by August 1942, but the slow delivery of Spitfires (Mk VCs, many of which had been diverted to the Middle East) meant that it was the middle of January 1943 before all three squadrons of No 1 Fighter Wing and their radar-equipped Mobile Fighter Sector HQ were operational in the Darwin area. No 1 Fighter Wing was commanded by Wing Commander Clive Caldwell, a highly skilled and experienced fighter pilot with 20 victories.

By the end of May 1943 the Spitfires had destroyed 24 enemy aircraft, but ten Spitfires had also been lost in combat, with others destroyed in forced landings. A change of tactics produced better results, and the Spitfires, which had been subjected to much criticism by the Australian media, began to inflict more serious punishment on the enemy. By the middle of the year 247 Spitfire VCs had been delivered to Australia, but such was the rate of attrition in No 1 Fighter Wing that no spare aircraft were available to form new squadrons until the Japanese air attacks began to lose momentum in late 1943, when No 79 Squadron RAAF was able to re-equip for operations in New Guinea.

In April 1944 the Australian Spitfire squadrons began to receive the more effective Mk VIII, which also equipped two more RAF squadrons, Nos 548

and 549 Squadrons, formed in Australia for air defence duties. Both became operational in April 1944. While the three RAF squadrons remained responsible for air defence, Nos 452 and 457 Squadrons moved forward to Morotai in the Moluccas in December 1944 and February 1945 as part of the First Tactical Air Force, RAAF, being followed by No 79 Squadron. The RAAF Spitfire squadrons disbanded shortly after the end of hostilities in August 1945. The RAF squadrons disposed of their aircraft in September and their personnel embarked for the UK in the following month. Only No 54 Squadron was destined to re-form as a fighter unit in the post-war years.

The Burma campaign

The first Spitfires (Mk VCs) in the Burma–India theatre became operational with Nos 136, 607 and 615 Squadrons (all former Hurricane units) in September 1943, and quickly made their mark by destroying four Mitsubishi Dinah fast reconnaissance aircraft within a month. On 31 December, No 136 Squadron destroyed 12 Japanese bombers and fighters of a force that was attempting to attack shipping off the Arakan coast. By this time two more Spitfire squadrons had arrived in India;

Above: **Spitfire VC of Squadron Leader E.M. Gibbs, OC No 54 Squadron, being pushed back into its camouflaged bay at Darwin, 22 June 1943.**

these were Nos 81 and 152, equipped with the Spitfire Mk VIII. By the beginning of 1944 there were six Spitfire squadrons on Eastern Air Command's order of battle; these were Nos 136 and 607 (No 165 Wing) at Ramu, still with Spitfire VCs; No 615 Squadron, also with VCs, at Dohazari with No 166 Wing; Nos 152 and 155 Squadrons at Bargacchi and Alipore, with Mk VIIIs; and No 81 Squadron at Tulihal, also with Mk VIIIs, responsible for covering the Imphal sector. In January 1944 the Spitfire squadrons claimed 24 enemy aircraft destroyed for the loss of seven Spitfires in air combat; their most numerous opponent was the Nakajima Ki-43 Hayabusa, known as Oscar to the Allies. But they were also encountering increasing numbers of the Mitsubishi A6M3 Model 32 fighter, an improved clipped-wing version of the Zero known as the Hamp.

Imphal

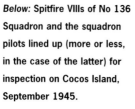

Below: **Spitfire VIIIs of No 136 Squadron and the squadron pilots lined up (more or less, in the case of the latter) for inspection on Cocos Island, September 1945.**

The arrival of the Spitfires was timely, for early in 1944 the Japanese launched a major offensive with the objective of breaking through to India. The fortified position of Imphal came under a siege that was to last for 80 days, during which time the Spitfire squadrons, operating from within the perimeter, kept enemy fighters away from the

transport aircraft that were bringing in supplies to the besieged troops. The plan was to keep three Spitfire squadrons available at Imphal at any one time, with a fourth in immediate support, and it worked well.

In general, the Spitfire pilots took advantage of the Mk VIII's superior performance at altitude to position themselves above enemy fighters, attack at speed out of the sun, then climb away hard out of range; these were much the same tactics that the Spitfire squadrons used in the defence of northern Australia. The Japanese Oscars, the only enemy fighter type encountered at Imphal, were more manoeuvrable than the Spitfire, had greater endurance, and were generally present in greater numbers, so the Spitfire pilots avoided turning combats wherever possible. Proof that the tactics were effective lay in the fact that in the entire 80-day siege, the enemy managed to shoot down only three transport aircraft.

By July 1944 there were ten Spitfire squadrons on the Burma front, Nos 17 and 273 Squadrons having been transferred there. The total included a PR squadron, No 681. Two of the squadrons, Nos 81 and 136, were withdrawn to Ceylon in July and August 1944. No 81 Squadron disbanded in June 1945, but No 136 deployed to the Cocos Islands

in March and, after the Japanese surrender in September, went to Kuala Lumpur in Malaya. It remained there until May 1946, when it moved to Bombay and was re-numbered as No 152 Squadron.

Of the other squadrons, No 615 went to Calcutta for air defence duties in August 1944, returning to Burma in February 1945 to operate in the tactical role with Nos 67, 152, 155 and 607 and Nos 1, 2, 3, 4, 6, 7, 8, 9 and 10 Squadrons of the Indian Air Force, now combat-ready and armed with the Spitfire VIII. All provided support for the Fourteenth Army in the closing phase of the Burma Campaign.

Far Eastern Seafires

In October 1943, the escort carrier HMS *Battler* arrived in the Indian Ocean to form the nucleus of an anti-submarine group.

Her air group consisted of a single squadron, No 834, which included a flight of Seafire Mk IIs. A few weeks later, a complete Seafire squadron, No 889, deployed to the theatre aboard the escort carrier HMS *Atheling*. But it was not until March 1945 that the Seafire reached the Indian Ocean in strength, three squadrons – Nos 807, 809 and 879 – being embarked on the escort carriers *Hunter*, *Stalker* and *Attacker*. These joined Royal Navy Hellcats in flying 180 combat air patrol (CAP) sorties in the course of Operation Dracula, the Allied amphibious landings in the Rangoon area. No Seafires were lost in combat, but six were written off in landing accidents.

Seafire ace

Seafires also served with the British Pacific Fleet, which operated under US command as Task Force 57, and made their first combat claims in the theatre on 1 April 1945. On that day Sub-Lieutenant R. Reynolds of No 894 Squadron, who had already destroyed two Blohm & Voss Bv 138 flying boats over the Atlantic, shot down three Zeros to become the only Seafire 'ace'. In their initial two-month operational deployment, the aircraft of Task Force 57 destroyed some 200 enemy aircraft, 98 in air combat and the rest in strafing attacks; most of the air combat victories were achieved by Corsairs and Hellcats, either over enemy territory or while flying on the outer CAP screen.

The Seafire's role was very much a secondary one, its lack of combat radius restricting it to operations in close proximity to the task force. But on the relatively few occasions when it did engage the enemy, it performed well. On 15 August 1945, for example, Seafires of Nos 887 and 894 Squadrons shot down eight Zeros in the Tokyo area; these were probably the last British air combat victories of World War II.

Above: This resplendent-looking Seafire, SW847, was one of 110 Mk XVs delivered to the Royal Navy, the majority of an original order for 500 being cancelled.

Below: The powerful Seafire 46 was the equivalent of the RAF's Spitfire F.22. Twenty-four were delivered, but none served on an aircraft carrier.

CHAPTER SIX

Foreign Spitfires and Spitfire Variants

In the immediate post-war years there was a thriving market for Spitfires in Europe and the Middle East, as many aircraft became surplus to RAF requirements. Spitfires served as first-line equipment with the air arms of some 20 countries, and played their part in several conflicts, most notably in the Arab-Israeli war of 1948–49, in which Spitfires fought Spitfires.

Opposite: Last and most powerful of the single-engined naval fighters, the Supermarine Seafang prototype shows its paces above the clouds.

Below: One of 51 Spitfire IXs handed over to the Belgian Air Force after World War II, this aircraft carries the civil registration OO-ARA.

Belgium

At the end of WWII there were two Belgian-manned Spitfire squadrons, Nos 349 and 350. These passed to the control of the Belgian Government in October 1956, together with 51 Spitfire Mk IXs and 25 Mk XVIs. The latter were on loan pending the delivery of Mk XIVs, ordered by the Belgians from Britain under the terms of the Western Union (the precursor of NATO). The Belgian Air Force took delivery of 132 Spitfire Mk XIVs between 1948 and 1951.

Burma

In 1951 the Union of Burma Air Force took delivery of 20 de-navalized Seafire Mk XVs, and in 1955 also received 30 Mk IXs from Israel.

Czechoslovakia

At the end of WWII there were three Czechoslovak Spitfire squadrons, Nos 310, 312 and 313. In August 1945 these flew to Czechoslovakia and were formally disbanded as RAF squadrons in 1946, forming the nucleus of a reconstituted Czech Air Force. They flew 75 Spitfire LFIXs, but these were retired when the country came under communist domination two years later. Many were purchased by Israel.

Denmark

In 1947-48 the Royal Danish Air Force took delivery of 41 Mk IX Spitfires and one Mk XI, the aircraft equipping three Eskadrille. The Spitfires were phased out between 1949 and 1955 as the RDAF's tactical fighter squadrons rearmed with Gloster Meteors and F-84 Thunderjets.

Egypt

The Royal Egyptian Air Force received 37 Spitfire Mk IXs between August and September 1946. Some of these saw action in the Arab-Israeli war of 1948-49, the only conflict in which Spitfire fought Spitfire (see under Israel). Twenty refurbished Spitfire F22s were also sold to Egypt in 1950, to be replaced later by Vampire FB5s.

Eire

Twelve de-navalized Seafire Mk IIIs, refurbished and returned to Spitfire VC standard, were delivered to the Irish Air Corps in 1947. The IAC also took delivery of six Mk IX trainers.

France

Six French-manned Spitfire squadrons served with the RAF in World War II. Between October 1945 and March 1946, 172 Spitfire Mk IXs were delivered to the Armée de l'Air from surplus RAF stocks, and many of these were immediately deployed to North Africa and French Indo-China. France also took delivery of 70 Mk Vs, most of which were used for training, and in 1948 the French Naval Air Arm received some Seafires, Mks III and XV, for service on the aircraft carrier *Arromanches* (formerly HMS *Colossus*).

Greece

At the end of the war in Europe, the operational component of the Royal Hellenic Air Force comprised Nos 335 and 336 Squadrons, armed with Spitfire Vs. A third Spitfire squadron, No 337, was formed shortly afterwards, and in 1947 the Spitfire Vs

Below: An Egyptian Air Force Spitfire LF.IX shot down during the War of Independence. It was later used for spare parts.

were replaced by Mk IXs. Deliveries of 74 of these aircraft were completed in 1949; they were followed by 55 Mk XVIs, which remained in service until 1955. One Spitfire PR Mk XI was also delivered.

India

In 1946 the Royal Indian Air Force was invited to deploy one of its Spitfire VIII squadrons, No 4, to Japan as part of the British Commonwealth Occupation Force. It was the last operational deployment of a RIAF Spitfire squadron, the others being in the process of conversion to the Tempest II. The last two Spitfire squadrons to receive Tempests, Nos 7 and 8, completed their conversion by the end of 1947, but two other squadrons, Nos 14 and 101, did not relinquish their Spitfires (Mks XVIII and PR.XIX) until 1955. No 14 Squadron rearmed with the Vampire FB9, while No 101 converted to a photo-recce version of the Vampire T55.

Below: Converted from a Mk IX, this Spitfire T.9 two-seat trainer was one of several delivered to the Indian Air Force.

Above: This Spitfire LF.IXE was flown by Ezer Weizmann, an experienced pilot who later rose to command the Israeli Air Force.

Below: Portugal took delivery of two batches of Spitfires, comprising 15 Mk IAs and 50 Mk VBs, in 1942 and 1943.

Israel

In 1948 the newly-created State of Israel purchased 50 Spitfire LF.IXs from Czechoslovakia, which was disposing of its stocks prior to rearming with Russian types. Nine more Spitfires were sent by the Czechs later, along with a substantial quantity of spares. Of the 59 Spitfires, 56 reached Israel and entered service. Prior to this, two Spitfires had been assembled from parts salvaged from abandoned British and crashed Egyptian aircraft, and these were put into service with No 101 Squadron, which took the ex-Czech Spitfires on charge as they arrived. The first kill was achieved by Jack Doyle, a Canadian WWII fighter pilot, who shot down an Egyptian Spitfire in an air battle over the Negev on 21 October 1948. Doyle destroyed a second Egyptian aircraft, a Fiat G.55, over Faluja on 28 December. Three days later, other 101 Squadron pilots destroyed two G.55s on the ground at Bir-Hama and a third in air combat. The fighting on Israel's southern frontier came to an end on 7 January 1949, but in a series of unfortunate incidents that day four RAF Spitfire FR.XVIIIs and a Tempest were shot down by 101 Squadron Spitfires, having infringed Israeli air space. Two of the British pilots were killed.

By the end of the War of Independence the Israeli Air Force had 26 Spitfires on strength, and 26 more aircraft were in the process of assembly, having arrived by sea. With more aircraft becoming available, a second Spitfire squadron, No 105, was established in August 1950. In 1953, 30 Spitfire IXs were acquired from Italy. A third Spitfire squadron, No 107, formed at the beginning of 1953 with aircraft released by No 101 Squadron, which was re-equipping with P-51D Mustangs. By 1955 all the surviving Spitfires were concentrated in No 105 Squadron, the last being withdrawn in February 1956. During the War of Independence some Israeli Spitfires operated in the reconnaissance role.

Italy

In 1947 Italy was limited by treaty to an air force consisting of not more than 200 fighters. At the time the Italian Air Force had about 110 Spitfire Mk IXs, and 30 of these aircraft were subsequently supplied to Israel.

Netherlands

One Dutch Spitfire Squadron, No 322, served as part of the RAF in World War II. Late in 1946 the Royal Netherlands Air Force took delivery of 55 ex-RAF Spitfire IXs, and also received a small number of XVIs.

Norway

The two Norwegian Spitfire squadrons that served in WWII were Nos 331 and 332, both of which made a significant contribution to 2nd TAF. In 1947 the Royal Norwegian Air Force purchased 30 Spitfire Mk IXs to equip these two units, further acquisitions bringing the total to 47. Both squadrons rearmed with the Republic F-84G Thunderjet in 1952–53.

Portugal

The Portuguese Air Force was an early overseas Spitfire customer, taking delivery of 15 Mk IAs in August 1943, together with some Hawker Hurricanes and

Westland Lysanders. This initial purchase was followed by 50 Spitfire VBs, most of which were also delivered in 1943. The Spitfire Vs remained in first-line service until 1952, when they were replaced by Republic P-47D Thunderbolts.

Sweden

In 1948, Sweden, faced with a growing threat from the Soviet Union, began to upgrade her armed forces, and between then and 1955 bought 50 PR.XIX Spitfires from surplus RAF stocks. Designated S31 in Swedish service, the Spitfires were operated by F11, a reconnaissance unit based at Nyköping. It is ironic that, at one point in World War II, the British Government attempted to bribe Sweden with an offer of 200 Spitfires if the Swedes would stop supplying ball bearings to the Germans.

Syria

Ten Spitfire F22s were delivered to Syria in 1950, drawn from surplus RAF stocks and refurbished by Airwork Ltd. They remained in first-line service until 1953, when they were replaced by Gloster Meteor F.8s.

Thailand

Thirty refurbished Spitfire XIVs were supplied to the Royal Thai Air Force from 1948, replacing a miscellany of elderly types left over from WWII. The Spitfires were replaced by Grumman F8F Bearcats in the mid-1950s.

Above: **Royal Swedish Air Force Spitfire PR.XIXs of F11. Fifty aircraft were purchased from surplus RAF stocks between 1948 and 1955.**

Below: **One of 30 Spitfire XIVs supplied to the Royal Thai Air Force from 1948, replacing a miscellany of elderly Japanese types.**

Right: Strange couple: a Turkish Air Force Spitfire VB formates with a Focke-Wulf Fw 190A-5. Turkey received 56 Spitfire VBs and 185 Mk IXs.

Turkey

This country was a major recipient of Spitfires while WWII was still in progress, taking delivery of 56 Mk VBs and 185 Mk IXs from 1943 onwards. The aircraft were sold to Turkey at nominal prices, the British government recognizing the need to keep her in a state of neutrality following the failure of diplomatic efforts to persuade her to join the Allied cause. The Germans supplied the Turkish Air Force with a number of Focke-Wulf Fw 190A-5s, the two types operating alongside one another until they were replaced by P-47D Thunderbolts in the late 1940s.

USSR

The first Spitfire operations from Russian territory took place in September 1942, when two PR.IVs of No 1 PRU deployed to North Russia to provide PR backup for possible air strikes against the *Tirpitz.* On 4 October, the Soviet Ambassador in London presented a request for the urgent delivery of Spitfires to relieve the pressure on the Stalingrad front; this was approved by Winston Churchill and early in 1943 137 Spitfire VBs drawn from Middle East stocks, plus 50 in spares form, were handed over to the Russians at Basrah in Iraq. These aircraft, armed with two cannon and two machine guns, were deployed with units of the 220th and 268th Fighter Divisions in time to take part in the major Soviet counter-attack that led to the encirclement and destruction of the German Sixth Army at Stalingrad.

In addition to the Mk Vs, the Russians also took delivery of 1188 Spitfire IXs before the end of the war, plus five PR Mk IVs and two PR Mk XIs. They fought on every front, but their main area of operations was in the north, where they performed excellent service in the air defence of Leningrad with the 26th Guards Fighter Regiment, and on the Karelian front.

Yugoslavia

Two Yugoslav-manned Spitfire squadrons served in the RAF in WWII, Nos 351 and 352, both in the Mediterranean theatre and the Balkans. No 351 operated Hurricanes but No 352 used Spitfire VCs, which continued to be used by Marshal Tito's embryo Yugoslav air arm for some time after the squadron disbanded in June 1945.

Below: Spitfire VCs of No 352 (Yugoslav) Squadron pictured in Italy, 1944. Its sister squadron, No 351, operated Hurricanes.

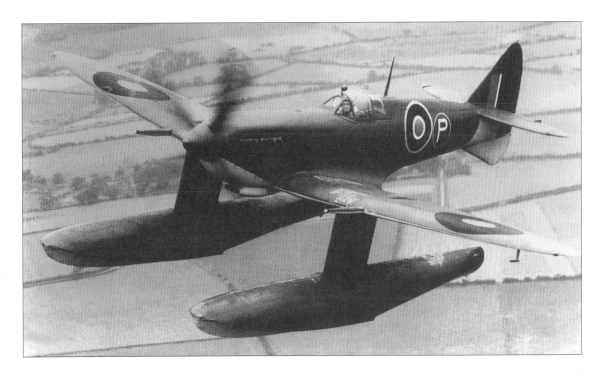

SPITFIRE DEVELOPMENTS

Spitfire floatplane (Supermarine Type 335)

In 1940, Spitfire Mk I R6772 was fitted with Blackburn Roc floats in response to a requirement for a fighter floatplane, mainly to operate from Norwegian fjords. A ventral fin was added to increase stability, but trials were generally unsatisfactory and the project was abandoned when the Norwegian campaign ended in defeat for the Allies. But the concept was revived in 1942, when the possibility was examined of establishing clandestine seaplane bases in the Aegean. A Spitfire VB was fitted with a set of floats designed by Supermarine and mounted on cantilever struts attached to the mainplane spars, the aircraft being converted by Folland Aircraft Ltd. The carburettor air intake was extended to avoid spray, a shorter-diameter propeller was fitted, and a ventral fin replaced the tailwheel.

The conversion was a success and the aircraft handled well, but for a marked tendency to yaw when the engine was throttled back (a tendency shared by the Spitfire landplane variants, although not to such an extent). Two Merlin 45-powered conversions, EP751 and EP754, were made by

Below: Converted from Spitfire XIV NN660, the prototype Vickers-Supermarine Spiteful was fitted with the Supermarine Type 371 laminar-flow wing.

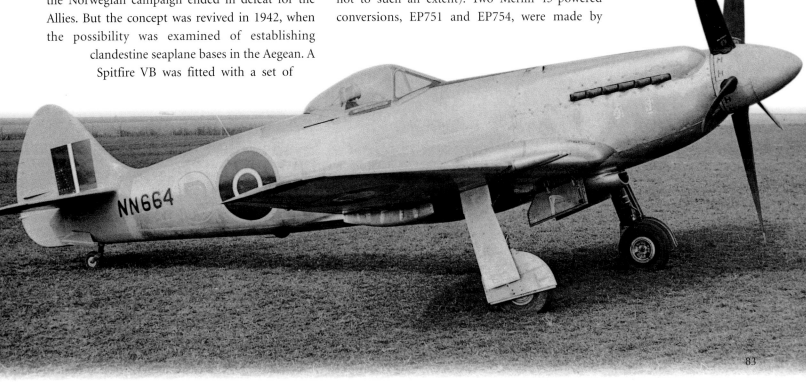

Folland, and later on an LF.IXB (Merlin 61 engine) was also converted, but the project was abandoned in 1943 when German forces occupied key Aegean islands in the wake of the Italian surrender. Six float conversion sets were also sent to the Middle East, where three Spitfires were fitted out and used for a time for the air defence of Alexandria. The Mk IX floatplane conversion had a maximum speed of 607km/h (377mph) at 6000m (19,700ft), making it the fastest floatplane in the world. With a 50-gallon auxiliary tank it had a range of 1240km (770 miles) at 362km/h (225mph) and 3050m (10,000ft).

Vickers-Supermarine Spiteful

Directly descended from the Spitfire, but bearing little resemblance to it except in profile, the Vickers-Supermarine Spiteful (Type 371) was designed to Air Ministry specification F1/43 and was in production by the end of World War II. The aircraft had a deeper fuselage than the Spitfire, a larger tailplane and an inward-retracting undercarriage. It also had a high-performance, laminar-flow wing. When F1/43 was issued, very little was known about transonic flight, the area roughly 30 per cent above and 30 per cent below the speed of sound. But experts in aerodynamics were making great efforts to design a wing that would persuade the air to flow more smoothly over a much greater area of the forward wing surface than before, delaying the breakdown of the airflow into the various forms of drag that produce turbulence.

The airflow actually passes over the wing in layers, the first of which, the boundary layer, remains stationary while successive ones progressively accelerate; this is known as laminar flow. The smoother the wing surface, and the more efficient its design, the smoother the airflow.

Below: This photograph of the prototype Supermarine Seafang clearly shows the shape of the laminar-flow wing, totally different from the Spitfire's graceful ellipse.

As combat aircraft reached speeds in the order of 725km/h (450mph), the airflow over the most curved parts of the aircraft accelerated locally to the speed of sound, causing compression that resulted in heavy drag. The aim of the high-speed, laminar-flow wing was to eliminate much of this, and in December 1942, by which time Supermarine had designed such a wing, three main objectives had been defined. These were to raise as much as possible the critical speed (Mach number) at which the buildup of drag due to compressibility became serious; to obtain a rate of roll faster than that of any existing fighter; and to reduce wing profile drag, so improving performance.

Numerous delays

The first of three Spiteful prototypes, NN660, crashed during the test flight programme. The other two aircraft, NN664 and NN667, differed in that the former had a short air intake under the fuselage, incorporating a tropical filter, whereas the latter had the intake directly aft of the propeller, cowled into the nose. NN664 flew for the first time in June 1944 in the hands of Vickers-Armstrong's test pilot Jeffrey Quill, who had been involved with the Spitfire test programme since its very beginning. Production of the Spiteful was subjected to numerous delays, and only 17 aircraft of 188 ordered were actually built. The first production model, RB515, was completed in March 1945, and the last aircraft was delivered on 17 January 1947. The first Spiteful to be taken on RAF charge was RB516, the sixth aircraft, which was delivered in November 1946. A few were retained by Supermarine for development purposes, and three went to various Ministry and Service experimental establishments; the rest were placed in storage at No 6 Maintenance Unit, RAF Brize Norton.

Unsuitable

Development of the Spiteful continued, the aircraft being designated F14 and powered by a 1772kW (2375hp) Griffon 69 engine fitted with a five-blade contra-rotating propeller. Most of the development work was carried out with NN664, and trials served only to underline the fact that the aircraft was unsuitable for squadron service, particularly in view

of its very tricky low-speed handling characteristics. It soon became obvious that the Spiteful did not, as had been expected, achieve a great advance on the later versions of the Spitfire, but the advantages of the new high-speed wing were demonstrated and put to good use in the design of the first generation of jet-propelled aircraft.

A new Griffon engine, the 89 or 90, and the addition of a six-bladed contra-rotating Rotol produced the Spiteful F15, while the sole F16 was powered by a Griffon 101 driving a five-bladed Rotol. This aircraft, RB518, was probably the fastest piston-engined aircraft ever, achieving a level speed of 795km/h (494mph) in 1947. This was only possible by using 25lb of boost pressure, which did the engine no good at all; on subsequent flights the aircraft had to force-land no fewer than seven times because of engine failure. The seventh time, at Chilbolton, its undercarriage legs were pushed up through the wings; it was then dropped from a great height by the salvage crane, bringing an inglorious end to its career. The Spiteful was declared obsolete in 1947, and passed into history.

Vickers-Supermarine Seafang

One of the Spitefuls, RB520, was fitted with an arrester hook to become the prototype of the naval version, the Seafang, produced to Specification N5/45. Before this, orders had already been placed for two new-build prototypes, VB893 and VB895, and 150 production aircraft. As it was, the production version appeared first, VG471 following the fifth Spiteful off the production line. This aircraft went to the Royal Aircraft Establishment on 15 January 1946, as the Seafang F31. As with the Spiteful, the Seafang did not show much improvement over the latest version of the Seafire, the F47. After the relative merits of the two types had been assessed the Admiralty called a halt to Seafang production after ten F31s and F32s (the latter having a Griffon 89 engine driving two three-bladed contra-rotating Rotol propellers, increased fuel capacity, and hydraulically operated folding wings that could be actuated while taxiing) had been delivered. Deck landing trials at Chilbolton and RNAS Ford were carried out by Lieutenant-Commander Mike Lithgow (later to become Supermarine's chief test pilot), and the conclusion was that the Seafang was suitable for carrier operations, with an approach speed of 95 knots, no tendency to float with the throttle closed, and good pilot visibility. By this time, however, the Admiralty had already placed a production order for another Supermarine design, the E10/44; this was to emerge as the Attacker, the Royal Navy's first jet fighter. The story of the Seafang ended with an attempt to sell the type to the Royal Netherlands Navy, which in the event selected the Fairey Firefly instead.

Above: **The aerodynamic experiments with the laminar flow wing were put to good use in the design of the Supermarine Attacker, the RN's first jet fighter.**

Appendices

SPITFIRE SQUADRONS

Squadron	Code	Spitfire Mks	Dates
1	JX	IXB	Apr 44–May 45
		F.21	May 45–Oct 46

(Converted to Meteor F.3s, October 1946)

2	OI	XIV	Nov 44–Jan 51
		XI	Sept 45–Jan 46
		XIX	Jan 46–Mar 51

(Began conversion to Meteor FR.9s from December 1950)

4	UP	XI	Jan 44–Aug 45

*(Disbanded at B.118 Celle, 31 August 1945; No 605
Squadron re-numbered 4 Squadron, 1 September 1945)*

5	OQ	LF.16E	Feb 48–Sept 51

*(Disbanded at Chivenor, 25 September 1951. Re-formed 1
March 1952 with Vampire FB.5s)*

6	JV	IX	Dec 45–Dec 46

(Converted to Tempest VIs, December 1946)

11	EX	XIV, XVIII	Jun 45–Feb 48

*(Disbanded at Miho, Japan, 23 February 1948. No 107
Squadron renumbered 11 Squadron, 4 October 1948)*

16	UG	XI	Sept 43–Sept 44
		XIX	Mar 45–Mar 46
		XIV	Oct 45–Mar 46
		XVI	Dec 45–Mar 46

*(Army Co-operation unit. Converted to Tempest Vs, April
1946)*

19	QV	I	Aug 38–Sept 40
		IIA	Sept 40–Oct 41
		VB/C	Oct 41–Aug 43
		IX	Aug 43–Feb 44
		LF.16E	Mar–Oct 46

*(Flew Mustangs, February 1944–March 1946. Converted to
Hornets, October 1946)*

20	HN	VIII	Sept–Dec 45
		XIV	Dec 45–May 46
26	XC	VA/B/C	Mar 44–Jan 45
		XI	Oct 45–Apr 46
		XIV	Jun 45–Jan 46

(Converted to Tempest F.2s, June 1946)

**Right: Tropicalized Mk VB
Spitfire AB320 in flight.**

Squadron	Code	Spitfire Mks	Dates
28	BF	IX	Jul–Oct 45
		VIII	Oct–Dec 45
		XIV	Oct 45–Feb 47
		FR.XVIII	Feb 47–Feb 51

(Converted to Vampire FB.5s, February 1951)

32	GZ	VC	Apr–Nov 43;
			May 44–Sep 45
		IX	Jun 43–Jul 44;
			Nov 44–Jun 47
		VIII	Dec 43–Jul 44
		F.XVIII	Jun 47–May 49

(Began conversion to Vampire F.3s, March 1949)

33	RS/5R	VB/C	Jan–Jun 43;
			Dec 43–Mar 44
		IXE	Apr–Dec 44
		XVIE	Nov 45–Oct 46

(Converted to Tempest F.2s, October 1946)

34	8Q	PR.XIX	Aug 46–Jul 47
		LF.XVIE	Feb 49–Mar 51

*(Disbanded at Palam, India, 30 July 1947. Re-formed 11
February 1949)*

41	EB	I	Jun 39–Nov 40;
			Mar–Apr 41
		IIA	Oct 40–Aug 41
		VB	Aug 41–Mar 43
		XII	Feb 43–Sept 44
		XIV	Sept 44–Apr 46
		F.21	Apr 46–Aug 47

*(Designated as No 12 Group's instrument flying training unit
with Oxfords and Harvards, August 1947–June 1948.
Converted to Hornets, June 1948)*

43	FT	VB/C	Feb 43–Jan 44
		VIII	Aug 43–Nov 44
		IX	Aug 43–May 47

*(Disbanded at Treviso, Italy, 16 May 1947. Re-formed with
Meteor F.4s, 11 February 1949)*

54	KL, DL	I	Mar 39–Feb 41
		IIA	Feb–Aug 41
		IIB	Nov 41–Mar 42
		VA	May–Aug 41
		VB	Jun–Nov 41;
			Mar–May 42
		VC	Sept 42–May 44
		VIII	Mar 44–Sept 45

(Converted to Tempest IIs, November 1945)

Squadron	Code	Spitfire Mks	Dates
56	US	IX	Apr–Jun 44

(Converted to Tempest Vs, June 1944)

60	MU	F.XVIII	Jan 47–Jan 51
		PR.XIX	Mar–Nov 50

(Converted to Vampire FB.5s, December 1950)

63	UB	VC	May 44–Jan 45
		LF.XVIE	Sept 46–Apr 48

(Converted to Meteor F.3s, April 1948)

64	SH	I	Apr 40–Feb 41
		IIA/B	Feb–Nov 41
		VB	Nov 41–Jul 42
		VC	Mar 43–Jul 44
		IX	Jul 42–Mar 43;
			Jul–Nov 44

(Converted to Mustangs, November 1944)

65	YT	I	Mar 39–Mar 41
		IIA/B	Mar–Oct 41
		VB/C	Oct 41–Aug 43
		IX	Aug 43–Jan 44
		XVIE	May 45–Sept 46

*(Operated Mustangs, December 1943–May 1945. Began
converting to Hornets, July 1946)*

66	LZ	I	Nov 38–Nov 40
		IIA	Nov 40–Feb 42
		VA/B/C	Feb 42–Nov 43
		IX	Nov 43–Nov 44
		XVI	Nov 44–Apr 45;
			Sep 46–Mar 47

(Converted to Meteor F.3s, March 1947)

67	RD	VIII	Feb 44–Aug 45

*(Disbanded at Akyab, Burma, August 1945. Re-formed 1950
with Vampire FB.5s)*

69	WI	PR.IV	Jun 41–Feb 43

*(Disbanded at Wahn on 6 November 1947. Re-formed as a
Canberra PR unit, May 1954)*

71	XR	IIA	Aug–Sept 41
		VB	Sept 41–Sept 42

*(First 'Eagle' squadron. Transferred to 4th Fighter Group,
USAAF, as 334th Fighter Squadron, 29 September 1942. No
71 Squadron re-formed in Oct 1950 as a Vampire FB.5 unit)*

72	RN	I	Apr 39–Apr 41
		IIA/B	Apr–Jul 41
		VB/C	Jul 41–Jan 44
		IX	Jul–Aug 42;
			Feb 43–Dec 46

(Converted to Vampire F.1s, February 1947)

73	TP	VC	Jun 43–Oct 44
		VIII	Jul–Nov 44
		IX	Oct 43–Nov 47
		F.22	Nov 47–Oct 48

(Began conversion to Vampire F.3s, August 1948)

Squadron	Code	Spitfire Mks	Dates
74	4D	I	Feb 39–Sept 40
		IIA	Sept 40–Jan 42
		VB	May–Jul 41;
			Nov 41–Apr 42
		VB/C	Aug 43–Apr 44
		IX	Oct 43–Apr 44
		IXE	Apr 44–Mar 45
		XVIE	Mar–May 45

(Flew Hurricanes, September 1942–September 1943. Converted to Meteor F.3s, June 1945)

80	W2	VC	Apr 43–Apr 44
		IX	Jul–Nov 43;
			May–Aug 44

(Converted to Tempest Vs, August 1944)

81	FL	VA	Jan–Apr 42
		VB	Apr–Oct 42
		VC	Nov 42–Nov 43
		IX	May–Jun 42;
			Jan–Nov 43
		VIII	Nov 43–Jun 45
		FR.XVIII	Aug 47–May 49
		PR.XIX	June 49–Apr 54

(Flew Thunderbolts, June 1945–June 1946, and Mosquitoes 1946. Began conversion to Meteor PR.10s, December 1953)

82	UX	PR.XIX	Oct 1946–Jan 52

(Carried out survey flights over W. Africa with Spitfires and Lancasters. Converted to Canberra PR.3s, November 1953)

87	LK	VB/C	Apr 43–Aug 44
		VIII	Jan–Aug 44
		IX	Jun 43–Dec 46

(Disbanded at Tisano, Italy, 30 December 1946. Re-formed 1952 as a night fighter squadron with Gloster Javelins)

91	DL	IIA	Jan–May 41
		VA/B	Mar 41–Apr 43
		XII	Apr 43–Mar 44
		XIV	Mar–Aug 44
		IXB	Apr 45–Oct 46

(Converted to Meteor F.3s, October 1946)

Squadron	Code	Spitfire Mks	Dates
92	QJ	I	Mar 40–Feb 41
		VB	Feb 41–Feb 42
		VB/C	Aug 42–Sept 43
		IX	Mar–Sept 43
		VIII	Jul 43–Dec 46
		IX	Jun–Dec 46

(Converted to Meteor F.3s, January 1947)

93	HN	VB/C	Jun 42–Aug 43
		IX	Jul 43–Sept 45

(Converted to Mustangs, January 1946)

94	GO	VB/C	Mar 44–Feb 45
		IX	Feb–Aug 44;
			Feb–Apr 45
		VIII	Feb–Apr 45

(Disbanded at Sedes, Greece, April 1945. Re-formed with Vampire FB.5s, 1950)

111	JU	I	Apr–May 41
		IIA	May–Sept 41
		VB	Aug 41–Oct 42
		VC	Nov 42–Jan 44
		IXC	Jun 43–May 47

(Disbanded at Treviso, Italy, 12 May 1947. Re-formed with Meteor F.8s, 1953)

118	NK	IIA	Mar–Sept 41
		VB	Sept 41–Jul 44
		IX	Jan 44–Jan 45

(Converted to Mustangs, January 1945)

121	AV	IIA	Oct–Nov 41
		VB	Nov 41–Sept 42

(Eagle Squadron. Transferred to USAAF as 335th FS, 4th FG, on 29 September 1942. Converted to P-47s, March 1943)

122	MT	IIA/B	May–Oct 41
		VB/C	Feb–Oct 42;
			May–Aug 43
		IX	Oct 42–May 43;
			Aug 43–Feb 44;
			Aug 45–Feb 46
		F.21	Feb–Apr 46

(Operated Mustangs, February 1944–August 1945. Re-numbered 41 Squadron, 1 April 1946)

Squadron	Code	Spitfire Mks	Dates
123	XE	I	May–Sept 41
		IIA	Sept 41–Jan 42
		VB	Jan–Apr 42
		VC	May–Oct 43

(Operated Hurricanes, November 1943–August 1944. Converted to P-47 Thunderbolts, September 1944)

124	ON	I	May–Oct 41
		IIA	Oct–Nov 41
		VB	Nov 41–Jul 42
		VI	Jul 42–Mar 43
		VII	Mar 43–Jul 44
		IX	Jul 44–Jul 45

(Converted to Meteor F.3s, July 1945. Re-numbered 56 Squadron, 1 April 1946)

126	5J	VC	Mar 42–Apr 44
		IX	Aug–Dec 43;
			May–Dec 44
		XVIE	Feb–Mar 46

(Also operated Mustangs, December 1944–March 1946. Disbanded at Hethel, Norfolk, on 10 March 1946)

127	9N	VC	Jan–Oct 43
		IX	Mar–Nov 44
		XVI	Nov 44–Apr 45

(Disbanded at B.106 Twente, 30 April 1945)

129	DV	I	Jun–Aug 41
		IIA	Aug 41
		VB/C	Aug 41–Jun 43
		VI	Dec 42–Jan 43
		IX	Jun 43–Apr 44;
			May 45–Sep 46

(Operated Mustangs April 1944–May 1945. Re-numbered 257 Squadron, September 1946)

130	PJ/AP	II	Jun–Oct 41
		VA/C	Oct 41–Aug 44
		XIV	Aug 44–May 45
		IX	May 45–Oct 46

(Converted to Vampire F.1s, October 1946)

Left: Spitfire LF IXEs of No 43 Squadron at Zeltweg, Austria in September 1945.

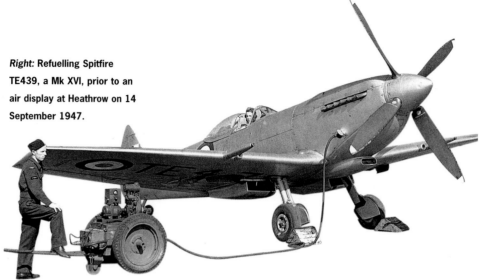

Right: Refuelling Spitfire TE439, a Mk XVI, prior to an air display at Heathrow on 14 September 1947.

Squadron	Code	Spitfire Mks	Dates
131	NX	I	Jul–Sept 41
		IIA	Sept–Dec 41
		VB/C	Dec 41–Sept 43
		IX	Sept 43–Mar 44
		VII	Mar–Nov 44
		VIII	Feb–Jun 45

(*Disbanded at Kuala Lumpur, Malaya, 10 June 1945; number transferred to 134 Squadron*)

132	FF	I	Jul–Nov 41
		IIB	Sept 41–Apr 42
		VB/C	Mar 42–Sep 43; Jan–Mar 44
		IXB	Sept 43–Jan 44; Mar–Jul 44
		IXE	Jul–Dec 44
		VIII	Jan–May 45
		XIV	May 45–Apr 46

(*Disbanded at Kai Tak, Hong Kong, 15 April 1946*)

133	MD	IIA	Oct 41–Jan 42
		VA	Jan–Mar 42
		VB	Feb–Sept 42
		IXC	Sept 42

(*Eagle squadron. Transferred to USAAF as the 336th FS, 4th FG, 29 September 1942*)

134	GQ	VA	Dec 41–Apr 42
		IIA	Jan–Feb 42
		VB/C	Jun 43–Aug 43

(*Also operated Hurricanes, 1943–44. Re-numbered 131 Squadron, 10 June 1945*)

136	HM	VC	Oct 43–Mar 44
		VIII	Jan 44–Feb 45; Apr 45–May 46
		XIV	Feb–May 46

(*Re-numbered 152 Squadron, May 1946*)

140	ZW	IV	Sept 41–Jan 44
		XI	Sept 43–Apr 44

(*PR unit, formed from 1416 Flight, 17 September 1941. Last Spitfire sortie flown on 27 April 1944; converted to Mosquitoes.*)

Squadron	Code	Spitfire Mks	Dates
145	ZX	IIA/B	Feb 41–Feb 42
		VA/B	Apr 42–Aug 43
		VIII	Aug 43–Aug 45
		IX	Jun 43–Aug 45

(*Disbanded at Treviso, Italy, 19 August 1945. Re-formed with Vampire FB.5s, March 1952*)

152	UM	I	Jan 40–Apr 41
		IIA	Apr 41–Feb 42
		VB/C	Feb 42–Nov 43
		IX	Aug–Nov 43
		VIII	Nov 43–Jul 46
		XIV	Jan–Jul 46

(*Converted to Tempest F.2s, July 1946*)

153	TB	VIII/IX	Aug–Sept 44

(*Primarily operated Beaufighters. Disbanded Reghaia, Algeria, 5 September 1944. Re-formed 7 October with Lancasters*)

154	HT	IIA	Nov 41–Mar 42
		VA/B	Feb 42–Jan 43
		VC	Jan 43–Apr 44
		IX	Jul 43–Sept 44
		VIII	Nov 44–Feb 45

(*Converted to Mustangs, February 1945. Disbanded at Calenzana, Italy, 31 March 1945*)

155	DG	VIII	Jan 44–Aug 46

(*Disbanded at Thedaw, Burma, 31 August 1946. Re-formed with Whirlwind helicopters, 1954*)

164	FJ	VA	Apr–Sept 42
		VB	Sept 42–Jan 43
		IXE	Jun 45–Aug 46
		XVIE	Jul–Aug 46

(*Operated Hurricanes, February 1943–March 1944, and Typhoons, January 1944–June 1945. Re-numbered 63 Squadron, 31 August 1946*)

165	SK	VA/B	Apr 42–Oct 43
		IX	Oct 43–Feb 45; Jun 45–Sep 46

(*Operated Mustangs, February–June 1945. Disbanded at Duxford, 1 September 1946*)

Squadron	Code	Spitfire Mks	Dates
183	HF	IX	Jun–Aug 1945

(*Converted to Tempest IIs, August 1945. Re-numbered 54 Squadron on 15 November 1945*)

184	BR	VB	Oct–Dec 43

(*Converted to Typhoons, December 1943*)

185	GL	VB/C	Feb 42–Sept 44
		VIII	Aug–Sept 44; Mar–Aug 45
		IX	Dec 43–Aug 45

(*Disbanded at Campoformido, Italy, 19 August 1945. Re-formed 1951 with Vampire FB.5s*)

186	AP	VB	Feb–Apr 44

(*Renumbered 130 Squadron, 5 April 1944*)

208	RG	VC	Dec 43–Jul 44
		VIII	Aug–Oct 44
		IX	Mar 44–Aug 46
		FR.XVIII	Aug 46–Mar 51

(*Converted to Meteor FR.9s, March 1951*)

213	AK	VC	Feb–May 44
		IX	Feb–Jun 44

(*Converted to Mustangs, May 1944*)

222	ZD	I	Mar 40–Mar 41
		IIA/B	Mar–Aug 41
		VB	Aug 41–May 43
		IX	May 43–Dec 44

(*Converted to Tempest Vs, December 1944*)

225	LX	VC	Jan 43–Jan 45
		IX	Jun 44–Jan 47

(*Disbanded at Campoformido, Italy, 7 January 1947*)

229	HB/9R	VC	Aug 42–Mar 44
		IX	Jan 43–Dec 44
		XVI	Dec 44–Jan 45

(*Re-numbered 603 Squadron, 10 January 1945*)

232	EF	VB	Apr 42–Feb 44
		IX	May 43–Oct 44

(*Disbanded at Naples, 31 October 1944. Re-formed as a transport squadron with Wellingtons, 15 November 1944*)

234	AZ/FX	I	Mar–Nov 40
		IIA	Nov 40–Sept 41
		VB/C	Sept 41–Sept 44
		VI	Mar–May 43
		IX	Aug 45–Feb 46

(*Operated Mustangs, September 1944–August 1945. Re-numbered 266 Squadron, 1 September 1946*)

237	Uncoded	VC	Dec 43–Mar 44
		IX	Mar 44–Dec 45

(*Re-numbered 93 Squadron, 1 January 1946*)

238	KC	VB/C	Jan 43–Apr 44
		IX	Sept 43–Oct 44
		VIII	Jun–Oct 44

(*Disbanded at Naples, 31 October 1944. Re-formed as a transport unit, 1 December 1944*)

241	RZ	VB	Feb–Mar 43
		IX	Dec 43–Aug 45
		VIII	Jan 44–Aug 45

(*Disbanded at Treviso, Italy, 14 August 1945*)

242	LE	VB/C	Apr 42–Apr 44
		IX	Jun 43–Oct 44

(*Disbanded while en route to N. Africa, 4 November 1944. Re-formed as a transport unit, 15 November 1944*)

Squadron	Code	Spitfire Mks	Dates
243	SN	VB	Jun–Sept 42
		VB/C	Jan 43–Mar 44
		IX	Jun 43–Sept 44

(Disbanded at Le Vallon, France, 30 September 1944. Re-formed as a transport unit, 15 December 1944)

249	GN	VB/C	Feb 42–Sept 44
		IX	Jun–Nov 43;
			Apr–Jun 45

(Operated Mustangs September 1944–April 1945. Disbanded at Brindisi, Italy, 16 August 1945)

253	SW	VC	Mar–Nov 44
		VIII	Nov 44–May 47
		XI	Mar–May 47

(Disbanded at Treviso, Italy, 16 May 1947. Re-formed at Waterbeach as a Venom night fighter squadron, 18 April 1955)

256	JT	VIII/IX	May–Aug 44

(Absorbed Spitfires of the Gibraltar Defence Flight. Disbanded at Nicosia, Cyprus, 12 September 1946. Re-formed with Meteor night fighters at Ahlhorn, November 1952)

257	FM	I	May–Jun 40
		VB	Apr–May 42

(Used Hurricanes June 1940–September 1942. Spitfire VBs used between relinquishing Hurricanes and converting to Typhoons)

266	UO	I	Jan 40–Apr 41
		IIA	Sept 40–Sept 41
		VB	Sept 41–May 42

(Began conversion to Typhoons, January 1942)

268	EG	XIVB	Apr–Sept 45
		XIX	Sept 45

(Re-numbered 16 Squadron, 19 September 1945. No 487 Squadron (Mosquitoes) re-numbered 268 Squadron, same day)

269	UA	VB	Feb 44–Mar 46

(Air-sea rescue squadron. One Spitfire flight for ASR escort)

273	MS	VIII	Mar 44–Jan 46
		XIV	Nov 45–Jan 46

(Disbanded at Saigon, 31 January 1946)

274	JJ	VB/C	Apr 43–Apr 44
		IX	May–Aug 44

(Converted to Tempest Vs, August 1944)

275	PV	VB	Jan–Apr 43;
			Apr 44–Feb 45

(Air-sea rescue squadron. One Spitfire flight for ASR escort)

276	VA	IIA	Apr–May 43
		VB	May 44–Feb 45

(ASR squadron. One Spitfire flight for ASR escort. Disbanded at Dunsfold, 14 November 1945)

277	BA	IIA	Dec 42–May 44
		VB	May 44–Feb 45

(ASR squadron. One Spitfire flight for ASR escort. Disbanded at Hawkinge, 15 February 1945)

278	MY	VB	Apr 44–Feb 45

(ASR squadron. One Spitfire flight for ASR escort. Disbanded at Thorney Island 14 October 1945)

287	KZ	VB	Nov 43–Mar 44
		IX	Nov 44–Aug 45
		XVIE	Jun 45–Jun 46

(Anti-aircraft co-operation squadron. Disbanded at West Malling, 15 June 1946)

Squadron	Code	Spitfire Mks	Dates
288	RP	IX, XVI	Nov 44–Jun 46
		LF.XVIE	Mar–Jul 53

(AAC squadron. Disbanded on 15 June 1946, but re-formed at Middle Wallop on 16 March 1953. Spitfires replaced by Boulton Baul Balliol T.2s)

289	YE	XVI	May–Jun 1945

(AAC squadron. Disbanded at Andover, 26 June 1945)

290	X6	VB	Dec 44–Oct 45

(AAC squadron. Disbanded at B.83 Knokke-le-Zoute, Belgium, 27 October 1945)

302	WX	VB/C	Oct 41–Sept 43
		IXC/E	Sept 43–Feb 45
		XVI	Feb 45–Dec 46

(Polish 'Poznanski' Squadron. Disbanded at B.111 Ahlhorn, 18 December 1946)

303	RF	I	Jan–Feb 41
		IIA	Feb–Oct 41
		VB	Oct 41–Jul 44
		IX	Jun–Nov 43;
			Jul 44–Apr 45
		XVI	Feb–Apr 45

(Polish 'Warsaw-Kosciusco' Squadron. Disbanded at Hethel, Norfolk, 11 December 1946)

306	UZ	IIB	Jul–Dec 41
		VB	Dec 41–Sep 42;
			Mar 43–Mar 44
		IX	Sept 42–Mar 43

(Polish 'Torunski' Squadron. Converted to Mustangs, March 1944. Disbanded at Coltishall, 6 January 1947)

308	ZF	I	Apr–May 41
		IIA/B	May–Sept 41
		VB	Sept 41–Nov 43
		IX	Nov 43–Mar 45
		XVI	Mar 45–Dec 46

(Polish 'Krakowski' Squadron. Disbanded at B.111 Ahlhorn on 18 December 1946)

310	NN	IIA	Oct–Dec 41
		VB/C	Nov 41–Feb 44;
			Jul–Aug 44
		VI	Jul–Sept 43
		IX	Jan 44–Feb 46

(Czechoslovak squadron. Disbanded at Prague, 15 February 1946)

312	DU	IIA	Oct–Dec 41
		VB/C	Dec 41–Feb 44
		IX	Jan 44–Feb 46

(Czechoslovak squadron. Disbanded at Prague, 15 February 1946)

313	RY	I	May–Aug 41
		IIA	Aug–Nov 41
		VB/C	Oct 41–Feb 44;
			Jul–Oct 44
		VI	Jun–Jul 43
		VII	Jul–Aug 44
		IX	Feb–Jul 44;
			Oct 44–Feb 46

(Czechoslovak squadron. Disbanded at Prague, 15 February 1946)

Squadron	Code	Spitfire Mks	Dates
315	PK	IIA	Jul–Aug 41
		VB/C	Aug 41–Nov 42;
			Jun 43–Mar 44
		IX	Nov 42–Jun 43

(Polish 'Deblinski' Squadron. Converted to Mustangs, March 1944; disbanded at Coltishall, 14 January 1947)

316	SZ	VB/C	Oct–Mar 43;
			Sept 43–Apr 44
		IX	Mar–Sept 43

(Polish 'Warszawski' Squadron. Converted to Mustangs, April 1944; disbanded at Hethel, 11 December 1946)

317	JH	VB	Oct 41–Sept 43
		IX	Sept 43–May 45
		XVI	May 45–Dec 46

(Polish 'Wilenski' Squadron. Disbanded at B.111 Ahlhorn, 18 December 1946)

318	LW	VB/C	Feb 44–Mar 45
		IX	Nov 44–Aug 46

(Polish 'Gdanskski' Squadron. Disbanded at Coltishall, 31 August 1946)

322	VL/3W	VB/C	Jun 43–Mar 44
		XIV	Mar–Aug 44
		IXB	Aug–Nov 44
		XVIE	Nov 44–Oct 45

(Dutch squadron. Disbanded at B.116 Wunstorf, 7 October 1945, but the number later revived for a squadron of the Royal Netherlands AF)

326	9I	VB/C	Dec 43–Apr 44
		IX	Dec 43–Nov 45

(French GC 2/7 'Nice' Squadron. Released to French command at Grossaschenheim, Germany, November 1945)

327	7E	VB/C	Dec 43–Apr 44
		VIII	Jul–Sept 44
		IX	Dec 43–Nov 45

(French GC 1/3 'Corse' Squadron. Released to French command at Stuttgart/Sersheim, November 1945)

328	S8	VB/C	Dec 43–Nov 44
		VIII	Aug 44–Apr 45
		IX	Dec 43–Nov 45

(French GC 1/7 'Provence' Squadron. Released to French command at Grossaschenheim, Germany, November 1945)

Left: Spitfire Mk V of 316 (Polish) Squadron.

Squadron	Code	Spitfire Mks	Dates
329	5A	VB/C	Feb–Mar 44
		IX	Feb 44–Nov 45
		XVI	Feb–Mar 45

(French GC 1/2 'Cigognes' Squadron. Disbanded at Fairwood Common on 17 December 1945)

Squadron	Code	Spitfire Mks	Dates
331	FN	IIA	Nov 41–Apr 42
		VB	Mar–Oct 42
		IX	Nov 42–Sept 45

(Norwegian squadron. Released to Royal Norwegian AF command at Stavanger, 21 November 1945)

Squadron	Code	Spitfire Mks	Dates
332	AH	VA/B	Jan–Nov 42;
			Apr–Aug 43
		IX	Nov 42–Sept 45

(Norwegian squadron. Released to Royal Norwegian AF command at Stavanger, 21 September 1945)

Squadron	Code	Spitfire Mks	Dates
335	FG	VB/C	Dec 44–Jul 46

(Hellenic squadron. Disbanded at Salonika, 31 July 1946)

Squadron	Code	Spitfire Mks	Dates
336	Uncoded	VB/C	Jan 44–Jul 46

(Hellenic squadron. Disbanded at Salonika, 31 July 1946)

Squadron	Code	Spitfire Mks	Dates
340	GW	IIA	Nov 41–Mar 42
		VB	Mar–Oct 42;
			Mar 43–Feb 44
		IXB	Oct 42–Mar 43;
			Jan 44–Feb 45
		XVIE	Feb–Nov 45

(French 'Ile-de-France' Squadron. Released to French AF command at B.152 Fassberg, 25 November 1945)

Squadron	Code	Spitfire Mks	Dates
341	NL	VB	Jan–Mar 43;
			Oct 43–Feb 44
		IXB	May–Oct 43;
			Feb 44–Mar 45
		XVI	Mar–Nov 45

(French GC 3/2 'Alsace' Squadron. Released to French command at B.152 Fassberg, 7 November 1945)

Squadron	Code	Spitfire Mks	Dates
345	2Y	VB	Mar–Sept 44
		IX	Sept 44–Apr 45
		XVI	Apr–Nov 45

(French GC 2/2 'Berry' Squadron. Released to French command at B.152 Fassberg, 21 November 1945)

Squadron	Code	Spitfire Mks	Dates
349	GE	VA/B	Jun 43–Feb 44
		VC	Oct 43–Feb 44
		IX	Feb 44–Feb 45;
			Apr–May 45
		XVI	May 45–Oct 46

(Belgian squadron. Operated Tempest Vs, February–April 1945. Released to Belgian AF command at B.152 Fassberg, 24 October 1946)

Squadron	Code	Spitfire Mks	Dates
350	MN	IIA	Nov 41–Apr 42
		VB	Feb 42–Dec 43;
			Mar–Jul 44
		VC	Mar–Jul 44
		IX	Dec 43–Mar 44;
			Jul–Aug 44
		XIV	Aug 44–Oct 46
		XVI	Aug–Oct 46

(First Belgian-manned fighter squadron in RAF. Released to Belgian AF command at B.152 Fassberg, 15 October 1946)

Squadron	Code	Spitfire Mks	Dates
352	Uncoded	VC	Jun 44–Jun 45

(Yugoslav squadron. Disbanded at Prkos, 15 June 1945)

Squadron	Code	Spitfire Mks	Dates
501	SD	I	Apr–Jun 41
		IIA	May–Sept 41
		VB/C	Sept 41–Jul 44
		IX	Nov 43–Jul 44
		LF.XIVE	Nov 46–Jan 49

(Operated Tempest Vs July 1944–April 1945. Converted to Vampire F.1s from November 1948)

Squadron	Code	Spitfire Mks	Dates
502	RAC	F.22	Jun 48–Jan 51

(Auxiliary AF squadron. Converted to Vampire FB.5s, January 1951)

Squadron	Code	Spitfire Mks	Dates
504	RAD	F.22	May 48–Oct 49

(Auxiliary AF squadron. Converted to Meteor F.4s, October 1949)

Squadron	Code	Spitfire Mks	Dates
519	Z9	VI	Aug 43–Jan 45
		VII	Oct 44–Dec 45

(Meteorological squadron. One flight of Spitfires. Disbanded at Leuchars, 31 May 1946)

Squadron	Code	Spitfire Mks	Dates
520	2M	V	Feb–Jun 44

(Meteorological squadron. One flight of Spitfires. Disbanded at Gibraltar, 25 April 1946)

Squadron	Code	Spitfire Mks	Dates
521	5O	V	Aug 42–Mar 43

(Meteorological squadron. One flight of Spitfires. Disbanded at Chivenor, 1 April 1946)

Squadron	Code	Spitfire Mks	Dates
527	WN	VB	Jul 44–Apr 46

(Radar calibration squadron. One flight of Spitfires. Disbanded at Watton, 15 April 1946)

Squadron	Code	Spitfire Mks	Dates
541	E/WY	IV/V	Oct 42–Jun 43
		IX	Nov 42–Jan 43
		XI	Dec 42–Oct 46
		XIX	May 44–Apr 45;
			Nov 47–Apr 51

(PR squadron. Began conversion to Meteor PR.10s, December 1950)

Squadron	Code	Spitfire Mks	Dates
542	Uncoded	IV	Oct 42–Apr 43
		VII	Nov 42–Apr 43
		X	Jul 44–Apr 45
		XI	Apr 43–Aug 45
		XIX	May 44–Apr 45

(PR squadron. Disbanded at Benson, 27 August 1945. Re-formed with Canberra PR.7s, May 1954)

Squadron	Code	Spitfire Mks	Dates
543	Uncoded	IV/V	Oct 42–Oct 43
		XI	Jun–Oct 43

(PR squadron. Disbanded at Benson, 18 October 1943. Re-formed 1 July 1955 with Vickers Valiant B(PR)1s)

Squadron	Code	Spitfire Mks	Dates
544	Uncoded	IV	Oct 42–Oct 43
		IX	Aug–Oct 43

(PR unit. Disbanded at Benson, 31 October 1945)

Squadron	Code	Spitfire Mks	Dates
548	TS	VIII	Apr 44–Oct 45

(Formed in Australia for air defence duties. Disbanded at Darwin, 9 October 1945)

Squadron	Code	Spitfire Mks	Dates
549	ZF	VIII	Apr 44–Oct 45

(Formed in Australia for air defence duties. Disbanded at Darwin, 9 October 1945)

Squadron	Code	Spitfire Mks	Dates
567	I4	VB	Jun–Sept 45
		XVI	Jul 45–Jun 46

(AAC squadron. Disbanded at West Malling, 16 June 1946)

Squadron	Code	Spitfire Mks	Dates
577	3Y	VB	Jun–Jul 45
		XVI	Jun 45–Jun 46

(AAC squadron. Disbanded at Castle Bromwich, 15 June 1946)

Squadron	Code	Spitfire Mks	Dates
587	M4	XVI	Jul 45–Jun 46

(AAC squadron. Disbanded at Tangmere, 15 June 1946)

Right: USAAF Spitfire Mk XIs of 14th Squadron pictured at Mount Farm in April 1944.

Squadron	Code	Spitfire Mks	Dates
595	7B	VB	Nov 44–Jul 45
		IX	Jul 45
		XII	Dec 44–Jul 45
		XVI	Sept 45–Feb 49
		F.21	Jun 48–Feb 49

(AAC squadron. Re-numbered 5 Squadron, 11 February 1949)

600	RAG	F.XIVE	Jul 46–Jun 48
		F.21	Apr 47–Nov 50
		F.22	Jun 48–Apr 50

(Auxiliary AF squadron. Began conversion to Meteor F.4s, March 1950)

601	UF/RAH	VB	Mar–Apr 42
		VB/C	May 42–Jan 44
		VIII	Jan–Jun 44
		IX	Jun 44–May 45
		LF.16E	Dec 46–Dec 49

(Auxiliary AF squadron. Disbanded at Bellaria, Italy, 7 May 1945. Re-formed 10 May 1946. Converted to Vampire F.3s, November 1949)

602	LO/RAI	I	May 39–Jun 41
		IIA	May–Jul 41
		VB/C	Jul 41–Oct 43
		VI	Sept–Nov 42
		IX	Oct 43–Nov 44
		XVI	Nov 44–May 45
		F.21	Apr 47–Jan 51
		F.22	Jun 48–Jan 51

(Auxiliary AF squadron. Disbanded at Coltishall, 15 July 1945. Re-formed 10 May 1946. Converted to Vampire F.3s, January 1951)

603	XT/RAJ	I	Sept 39–Nov 40
		IIA	Oct 40–May 41
		VA/B	May 41–Apr 42
		VC	Apr–Aug 42
		XVI	Jan–Aug 45; Jun 46–Jun 48
		F.22	Jun 48–Jul 51

(Auxiliary AF squadron. Operated Beaufighters, 1943–44. Disbanded at Turnhouse 15 August 1945. Re-formed 10 May 1946. Converted to Vampire FB.5s, May 1951)

| 604 | RAK | LF.16E | Aug 46–May 50 |

(Auxiliary AF squadron. Night fighter squadron in WWII. Disbanded at B.51 Lille-Vendeville, 18 April 1945. Re-formed 10 April 1946. Began conversion to Vampire F.3s, November 1949)

607	AF/RAN	VC	Sept 43–Mar 44
		VIII	Mar 44–Jul 45
		XIV	Nov 46–Mar 49
		F.22	Jul 47–Jun 51

(Auxiliary AF squadron. Disbanded at Mingaladon, Burma, 31 July 1945. Re-formed 10 May 1946. Converted to Vampire FB.5s, June 1951)

| 608 | RAO | F.22 | Aug 48–Jun 51 |

(Auxiliary AF squadron. Began converting to Vampire F.3s, December 1949)

609	PR	I	Aug 39–May 41
		IIA	Feb–May 41
		VB/C	May 41–May 42
		LF.16E	Apr 48–Feb 51

(Auxiliary AF squadron. Operated Typhoons, April 1942–September 1943 and Mosquito NF30s, 1947–48. Began conversion to Vampire FB.5s, November 1950)

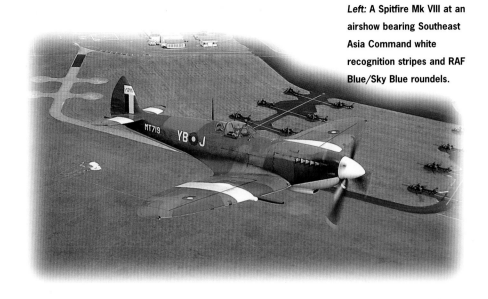

Left: **A Spitfire Mk VIII at an airshow bearing Southeast Asia Command white recognition stripes and RAF Blue/Sky Blue roundels.**

Squadron	Code	Spitfire Mks	Dates
610	DW/RAQ	I	Sept 39–Feb 41
		IIA/B	Feb–Jul 41
		VB/C	Jul–Aug 41; Nov 41–Mar 44
		XIV	Dec 43–Mar 45; Feb 47–Feb 50
		F.22	Sept 49–Feb 51

(Auxiliary AF squadron. Disbanded at Warmwell, 3 March 1945. Re-formed 10 May 1946. Converted to Meteor F.4s, April 1951)

611	FY/RAR	I	May 39–Mar 41
		IIA/B	Aug 40–Jun 41; Nov 41–Feb 42
		VB/C	Jun–Nov 41; Feb–Jul 42; Jul 43–Jul 44
		IX	Jul 42–Jul 43; Jul 44–Mar 45
		VII	Oct–Dec 44
		XIV	Nov 46–May 48
		F.22	Jun 48–Jun 51

(Auxiliary AF squadron. Operated Mustangs January–August 1945. Disbanded at Peterhead, Scotland, 15 August 1945. Re-formed 10 May 1946. Converted to Meteor F.4s, May 1951)

| 613 | Q3 | XIV | Feb 47–Dec 48 |
| | | F.22 | Jul 48–Mar 51 |

(Auxiliary AF squadron. Re-numbered 69 Squadron, 7 August 1945. Re-formed as 613 at Ringway, 10 May 1946. Converted to Vampire FB.5s, February 1951)

| 614 | RAU/7A | LF.XVIE | Jun 46–Jul 48 |
| | | F.22 | Jul 48–Jul 50 |

(Auxiliary AF squadron. Bomber squadron in WWII. Re-formed 10 May 1946. Converted to Vampire F.3s, July 1950)

615	KW/RAV	VC	Oct 43–Aug 44
		VIII	Jun 44–Jun 45
		XIV	Oct 46–Jan 49
		F.21	Jan 47–Jul 50
		F.22	Jul 48–Sept 50

(Auxiliary AF squadron. Disbanded at Cattack, India, 10 June 1945, and number transferred to 135 Squadron. Re-formed 10 May 1946. Converted to Meteor F.4s, September 1950)

Squadron	Code	Spitfire Mks	Dates
616	YQ/RAW	I	Oct 39–Feb 41
		IIA/B	Feb–Jul 41
		VB	Jul 41–Oct 42
		VI	Apr 42–Dec 43
		VII	Sept 43–Aug 44

(Auxiliary AF squadron. Converted to Meteor F.1s, July 1944. Disbanded at B.158 Lubeck, 29 August 1945. Re-formed 10 May 1946. Received Mosquito NF30s, September 1947, then Meteor F.3s, December 1948. No 616 was the RAF's first jet squadron)

| 631 | 6D | XVI | Jun 45–Feb 49 |

(AAC squadron. Re-numbered 20 Squadron, 7 February 1949)

| 667 | U4 | XVI | Jul–Dec 45 |

(AAC squadron. Disbanded at Gosport, 20 December 1945)

680	Uncoded	IV/V	Feb 43–Jun 44
		VI	Mar–Aug 43
		XI	Aug 43–Jul 46

(PR squadron. Relinquished Spitfires in July 1946 and became entirely equipped with Mosquitoes. Re-numbered 13 Squadron, 1 September 1946)

681	Uncoded	IV	Jan–Sept 43
		XI	Sept 43–Apr 46
		XIX	Jul 45–Aug 46

(PR squadron, formed from No 3 PRU at Dum Dum, India, January 1943. Re-numbered 34 Squadron, 1 August 1946)

682	Uncoded	IV	Feb–Dec 43
		XI	Feb 43–Sept 45
		XIX	Jun 44–Sept 45

(PR squadron, formed from No 4 PRU at Maison Blanche, Algeria, 1 February 1943. Disbanded at San Severo, Italy, 14 September 1945)

683	Uncoded	IV	Feb–Jul 43
		XI	Apr 43–Sept 45
		XIX	Sept 44–Sept 45

(PR squadron, formed from 'B' Flight, 69 Squadron, Luqa, Malta, on 8 February 1943. Disbanded at San Severo, Italy, 21 September 1945. Re-formed as a survey unit with Lancasters, 1950–53)

Squadron	Code	Spitfire Mks	Dates
691	5S	XVI	Aug 45–Feb 49

(AAC squadron. Re-numbered 17 Squadron, 11 February 1949)

Squadron	Code	Spitfire Mks	Dates
695	4M	VB	Sept 44–Jul 45
		XVI	Jul 45–Feb 49

(AAC squadron. Re-numbered 34 Squadron, 11 February 1949)

Squadron	Code	Spitfire Mks	Dates
1435	Uncoded	VB/C	Aug 42–Nov 43
		VC	May–Sept 44
		IX	Mar 43–Apr 45

(Formed from 1435 (Fighter Defence) Flight, Luqa, Malta on 2 August 1942. Disbanded at Gragnano Camp, Italy, 26 April 1945)

COMMONWEALTH SPITFIRE SQUADRONS

Squadron	Code	Spitfire Mks	Dates
400 RCAF	SP	XI	Apr 44–Jul 45

(Formed March 1941. Previously operated Lysanders, Tomahawks and Mustangs. Disbanded July 1945)

Squadron	Code	Spitfire Mks	Dates
401 RCAF	YO	IIA	Feb–Sept 41
		V	Sept 41–May 43
		IX	May 43–Oct 44
		XIV	Oct 44–June 45

(Arrived in UK June 1940; originally designated 1 Squadron RCAF; disbanded July 1945)

Squadron	Code	Spitfire Mks	Dates
402 RCAF	AE	VB	1942–43
		IX	1943–44
		XIV	1944–45

(Formed November 1940; disbanded 2 July 1945. Previously operated Hurricanes))

Squadron	Code	Spitfire Mks	Dates
403 RCAF	KH	V	Aug 41–Dec 42
		IX	Dec 42–Nov 43
		IXE	1944–45
		XVI	1945–45

(Formed 1 March 1941; disbanded 30 June 1945)

Squadron	Code	Spitfire Mks	Dates
411 RCAF	DB	I	Jan–Dec 41
		II	1941–42
		V	1942–43
		IX	1944–46

(Formed 15 June 1941; disbanded 21 March 1946)

Squadron	Code	Spitfire Mks	Dates
412 RCAF	VZ	II	Jul 41–Oct 43
		V	1943–44
		IX	1944–Mar 46

(Formed June 1941; disbanded March 1946)

Squadron	Code	Spitfire Mks	Dates
414 RCAF	RU	IX	Aug 44–Apr 45
		XIV	Apr–Aug 45

(Formed August 1941; disbanded August 1945. Previously used Tomahawks, Lysanders and Mustangs)

Squadron	Code	Spitfire Mks	Dates
416 RCAF	DN	II	Nov 41–Jul 42
		V	Jul–Dec 42
		IX	Dec 42–Oct 44
		XIV	Nov 44–Mar 46

(Formed 18 November 1941; disbanded 19 March 1946)

Squadron	Code	Spitfire Mks	Dates
417 RCAF	AN	II	Nov 41–Jan 43
		VC	Jan–Feb 43
		VIII	Aug 43–Apr 45
		IX	Apr–May 45

(Formed 27 November 1941; disbanded 1 July 1945)

Squadron	Code	Spitfire Mks	Dates
421	AU	V	Apr 42–May 43
		IX	May 43–Dec 44
		LF.XVI	Dec 44–Jul 45

(Formed 9 April 1942; disbanded 23 July 1945)

Squadron	Code	Spitfire Mks	Dates
430 RCAF	G9	XII	Sept 44
		XIV	Sept 44–Aug 45

(Formed 1 January 1943; disbanded 7 August 1945. Armed with Mustangs to September 1944)

Squadron	Code	Spitfire Mks	Dates
441 RCAF	9G	V	Feb–Oct 44
		IX	Oct 44–Aug 45

Squadron	Code	Spitfire Mks	Dates
442 RCAF	Y2	V	Feb–Oct 44
		IX	Oct 44–Aug 45

Squadron	Code	Spitfire Mks	Dates
443 RCAF	2I	V	Feb–Oct 44
		IX	Oct 44–Apr 45
		XVI	Apr 45–Jan 46
		XIV	Jan–Mar 46

(Formed 8 February 1944; disbanded 15 March 1946)

Squadron	Code	Spitfire Mks	Dates
451 RAAF	NI	V	Feb–Dec 43
		IX	Dec 43–Jan 45
		XIV	Jan 45–Feb 46

(Formed in the Middle East, 1941; disbanded February 1946)

Squadron	Code	Spitfire Mks	Dates
452 RAAF	UD	I	Apr–Oct 41
		II	Oct 41–Jan 42
		V	Jan 42–44

(Transferred from UK to Australia, 1942)

Squadron	Code	Spitfire Mks	Dates
453 RAAF	FU	V	Jun 42–Apr 43
		IX	Apr 43–Oct 44
		XVI	Oct 44–May 45

(Formed June 1942; disbanded 31 May 1945)

Squadron	Code	Spitfire Mks	Dates
457 RAAF	BP	II	Jun–Sept 41
		V	Sept 41–Jul 43
		IX	Jul 43–Aug 45

(Formed 16 June 1941; transferred to Australia, June 1942)

Squadron	Code	Spitfire Mks	Dates
485 RNZAF	OU	II	Mar–Nov 41
		V	Nov 41–Jul 43
		IX	Jul 43–Aug 45

(Formed March 1941, disbanded August 1945)

USAAF SPITFIRE SQUADRONS

Squadron	Code	Spitfire Mks	Dates
334th	QP	IXC	Sept 42–Mar 43

(4th Fighter Group. Rearmed with P-47s, March 1943. Formerly No 71 Eagle Squadron RAF)

Squadron	Code	Spitfire Mks	Dates
335th	AV	VB	Sept 42–Mar 43

(4th Fighter Group. Rearmed with P-47s, March 1943. Formerly No 121 Eagle Squadron RAF)

Squadron	Code	Spitfire Mks	Dates
336th	MD	IXC	Sept 42–Mar 43

(4th Fighter Group. Rearmed with P-47s, March 1943. Formerly No 133 Eagle Squadron RAF)

Squadron	Code	Spitfire Mks	Dates
307th	MX	VB/C	Jun 42–Apr 44

(31st Fighter Group. Assigned to Mediterranean theatre, November 1942. Rearmed with P-51s, April 1944)

Squadron	Code	Spitfire Mks	Dates
308th	HL	VB/C	Jun 42–Apr 44

(31st Fighter Group. Assigned to Mediterranean theatre, November 1942. Rearmed with P-51s, April 1944)

Squadron	Code	Spitfire Mks	Dates
309th	WZ	VB/C	Jun 42–Apr 44

(31st Fighter Group. Assigned to Mediterranean theatre, November 1942. Rearmed with P-51s, April 1944)

Squadron	Code	Spitfire Mks	Dates
2nd	QP	VB/C	Jun 42–May 44

(52nd Fighter Group. Assigned to Mediterranean theatre, November 1942. Rearmed with P-51s, May 1944)

Squadron	Code	Spitfire Mks	Dates
4th	WD	VB/C	Jun 42–May 44

(52nd Fighter Group. Assigned to Mediterranean theatre, November 1942. Rearmed with P-51s, May 1944)

Squadron	Code	Spitfire Mks	Dates
5th	VF	VB/C	Jun 42–May 44

(52nd Fighter Group. Assigned to Mediterranean theatre, November 1942. Rearmed with P-51s, May 1944)

Squadron	Code	Spitfire Mks	Dates
12th	ZM	VB	1942–44

(67th Reconnaissance Group)

Squadron	Code	Spitfire Mks	Dates
107th	AX	VB	1942–44

(67th Reconnaissance Group

Squadron	Code	Spitfire Mks	Dates
109th	VX	VB	1942–44

(67th Reconnaissance Group)

Squadron	Code	Spitfire Mks	Dates
153rd	ZS	VB	1942–44

(67th Reconnaissance Group)

Note: The 67th RG deployed to the European theatre in August 1942 and was assigned first to the Eighth and then (in October 1943) to the Ninth AF. In addition to Spitfires, it also used P-38s, P-51s and F-5s)

Right: Battle of Britain Memorial Flight Spitfire Mk XIX.

Left: **A Seafire battles the mud at a repair and salvage unit in Normandy, July 1944.**

OPERATIONAL SEAFIRE SQUADRONS

Squadron	Code	Spitfire Mks	Dates
800		XV/XV11	Oct 46–Apr 49
		FR.47	1949–51

(Previously armed with Hellcats. FR.47s saw action in Malaya and Korea)

Squadron	Code	Spitfire Mks	Dates
801		IB	Sept 42–May 43
		II	May 43–Feb 44
		III	1944–45

(Operated from HMS Furious during Tirpitz strikes, 1944; HMS Implacable in Pacific. Re-armed with Hawker Sea Fury)

802		XV	1945
		XV/XVII	1945–May 48

(Previously armed with Martlets. Re-armed with Sea Fury, 1948)

803		XV	Jun 45–May 46
		XVII	1946

(Previously armed with Fairey Fulmars)

804		XV	Oct 46–Jan 48
		FR.47	Feb 48–Aug 49

(Previously armed with Hellcats. Re-armed with Sea Fury, 1949)

805		III	Jul 45
		XV	Jan–May 46
		XVII	Apr 47–Aug 48

(Served with Royal Australian Navy. Operated Sea Furies from HMAS Sydney in Korean War)

806		XV	1945–46

(Previously armed with Fulmars)

807		IB	Jun 42–1943
		II/III	1944–45
		XVII	Dec 45–Aug 47

(Took part in Operation Torch, November 1942 (HMS Furious), invasion of Sicily 1943 (HMS Indomitable), Salerno landings 1943 (HMS Battler), invasion of southern France 1944 (HMS Hunter). Re-armed with Sea Fury, 1947; operated from HMS Theseus in Korean War)

808		IB	Dec 42–43
		III	1943–44

(Re-armed with Hellcats, 1944)

809		I	Jun 42–43
		II/III	1943–45

(Salerno landings, 1943 (HMS Unicorn); invasion of southern France, 1944 (HMS Stalker); Indian Ocean, 1944–45 (HMS Stalker)

833		II/III	Jun–Dec 43

(Battle of the Atlantic, HMS Stalker/HMS Activity. Mixed Seafire and Swordfish squadron)

834		II/III	Apr 43–44

(Battle of the Atlantic, HMS Hunter. Mixed Seafire/Swordfish squadron)

842		IIC	Jul 43–44

(Battle of the Atlantic, HMS Fencer. Mixed Seafire/Swordfish squadron)

851		III	Apr–May 44

(Re-armed with Avengers and Wildcats, 1944)

879		IIC	Mar 43–44
		III	1945

(Mediterranean and Aegean, HMS Attacker, 1944; Indian Ocean, HMS Attacker, 1945)

880		I	Aug–Dec 42
		II	Jan 43–45

(Operation Torch, November 1942, HMS Argus; invasion of Sicily, July 1943, HMS Indomitable; Salerno landings, September 1943, HMS Stalker; Tirpitz strikes, 1944, HMS Furious; shipping strikes in Norwegian waters, 1944, HMS Implacable; Pacific Fleet, HMS Implacable, 1945)

883		XVII	Sept 45–Feb 46

(Operated 25 aircraft prior to handing over to Royal Canadian Navy)

884		II	Nov 42–43

885		I/II	Sept 42–Nov 43
		III	Feb 44–45

886		II	Mar 43–44
		III	1944

(Salerno landings, 1943, HMS Attacker; Battle of the Atlantic, HMS Attacker, 1943–44)

887		I/II	Dec 42–43
		II	1943–44
		III	1945–Mar 46

(Salerno landings, 1943, HMS Unicorn; Battle of the Atlantic, 1944, HMS Unicorn; Tirpitz strikes, 1944, HMS Indefatigable; shipping strikes in Norwegian waters, 1944, HMS Indefatigable; Indian Ocean and Pacific, 1944–45, HMS Indefatigable)

889		III	1944

(Indian Ocean, 1944, HMS Atheling)

894		IIC	Mar 43–44
		III	1944–Mar 46

(Salerno landings, 1943, HMS Illustrious/HMS Unicorn; Tirpitz strikes, 1944, HMS Indefatigable; shipping strikes in Norwegian waters, 1944, HMS Implacable; Indian Ocean and Pacific, 1944–45, HMS Indefatigable)

895		IIC	Apr 43

897		I	Aug–Sept 42
		II	Apr 43–44
		III	1944

(Salerno landings, 1943, HMS Unicorn)

899		II	Jan 43
		III	1943–45

(Invasion of Sicily, 1943, HMS Indomitable; Salerno landings, September 1943, HMS Hunter; invasion of southern France, August 1944, HMS Khedive)

1831		F.XVII	Jun 47–Aug 51
1832		F.XVII	Jul 47–Nov 51
1833		F.XVII/FR.47	Aug 47–Jan 52

Spitfire Variants

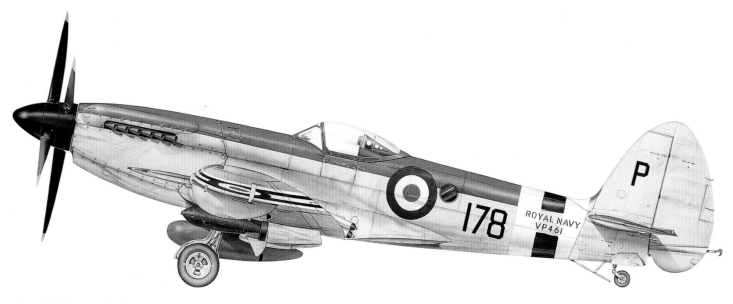

The Spitfire prototype

The Spitfire prototype, K5054, adapted to meet the requirements of Air Ministry Specification F.37/34, first flew on 5 March 1936, powered by a Rolls-Royce Merlin 'C' engine. It was first revealed publicly in a flypast at the Royal Air Force pageant, Hendon, on 27 July 1936. By October 1938, K5054 had been brought up to full Mk I standard. It survived several accidents during its test career, but was damaged beyond repair when it overturned in a landing accident at Farnbrough on 4 September 1939. The remains were stored at Farnborough for some time before being broken up, date unrecorded.

The High Speed Spitfire

In 1937, it was decided to use a Spitfire in an attempt to establish a new World Landplane Speed Record. Two Merlin II engines were modified to racing configuration, being tuned to produce 2000hp for a short period with the aid of special fuel (20% straight-run petrol, 60% benzol, 20% methanol and 3.3cc lead per US gallon). A Mk I airframe, K9834, was modified, its wing span being reduced and a revised cockpit canopy fitted, and featuring a four-bladed propeller. First flown on 10 November 1938, resplendent in high gloss blue with a silver trim and registered N17, it reached 656km/h (408mph), but could not surpass the speed of 755.138km/h (469.22mph) attained by Messerschmitt's Me 209 in April 1939. Fitted with a Merlin XII engine, K9834 was

allocated to the PRU on 24 November 1940 and served as its communications aircraft throughout the war, being stricken off charge on 21 May 1946.

Spitfire Mk I (Supermarine Type 300)

The first production Spitfire I, K9787, flew in May 1938. The first to enter service was K9789, the third production aircraft, which went to No 19 Squadron at Duxford on 4 August 1938 and went through 240 hours of intensive flying. In all, 1533 Mk Is were built by Supermarine and 50 more by Westland Aircraft. All Mk Is were declared obsolete in February 1945.

Spitfire Mk II (Supermarine Type 329)

The Mk II Spitfire was basically a Mk I built exclusively at the Castle Bromwich factory of Vickers-Armstrongs. Equipment was similar to that of the Mk I, with the addition of a Merlin XII engine developing 1175hp. Production totals were 750 Mk IIAs and 170 Mk IIBs (the A and B suffixes denoted armament variations). Some 50 aircraft, originally designated IICs, were fitted out for air-sea rescue work, equipped with a dinghy and with other survival gear stowed in the parachute flare chutes; these were redesignated Spitfires ASR.II in 1942.

Spitfire Mk III (Supermarine Type 330)

The Spitfire Mk III was intended to be a refined successor to the Mks I and II, with a 1390hp Merlin XX engine, clipped wings, retractable

tailwheel and other refinements. Two aircraft were built (N3297 and W3237), but the variant did not enter production, being used for experimental purposes.

Spitfire Mk IV (Supermarine Type 337)

The Mk IV was the first Griffon-engined Spitfire, and was a modified Mk IIB, DP845. This flew for the first time on 27 November 1941, but did not proceed beyond the experimental stage. The aircraft bore no relation to the PR.Mk.IV.

Spitfire PR.Mk IV

The Spitfire PR.IV, 229 of which were converted from MK VA/B airframes, was the main photo-reconnaissance type of the mid-war years. The variant used all the Merlin engine variants applicable to the Mk V, but the Merlin 45 and 46 were the recognized standard. The last PR.IV was withdrawn from service in February 1945.

Spitfire Mk V (Supermarine Type 349)

Converted from Mk I and II airframes, the Mk V, which began to reach the squadrons in March 1941, was to be the major Spitfire production version, with 6479 examples completed. It was produced in six different variants (F.VA/B/C and LF/VA/B/C), developed for high- and low-altitude roles. The majority of Spitfire Vs were armed with two 20mm cannon and four machine guns, affording a greater chance of success against armour plating. The Mk V was powered by a

Rolls-Royce Merlin 45 engine, developing 1415 hp at 5800m (19,000ft) against the 1150hp of the Merlin XII fitted in the Mk II. Nevertheless, the Mk V was essentially a compromise aircraft, rushed into service to meet an urgent Air Staff requirement for a fighter with a performance superior to that of the latest model of Messerschmitt. The debut of the Spitfire V came just in time, for in May 1941 the Luftwaffe fighter units began to receive the Messerschmitt Bf 109F, its service debut having been delayed through technical problems. The Spitfire V, however, failed to provide the overall superiority Fighter Command needed so badly. At high altitude, where many combats took place, it was found to be inferior to the Bf 109F on most counts, and several squadrons equipped with the Mk V suffered heavy losses. It was completely outclassed by the Focke-Wulf Fw 190. The Mk V was declared obsolete for RAF purposes in September 1945, but stocks were retained until March 1948.

Spitfire Mk VI (Supermarine Type 350)

The Spitfire Mk VI was developed specifically to counter enemy high-altitude reconnaissance aircraft, notably the Junkers Ju 86P. It was basically a Mk V airframe with a pressurized cabin, extended wingtips, a Merlin 47 engine and a four-bladed propeller for greater efficiency at height. One hundred examples were produced, one flight being attached to each home defence squadron of RAF Fighter Command. The Mk VI's service ceiling was 12,200m (40,000ft).

Spitfire Mk VII (Supermarine Type 351)

The Mk VII, also with a pressurized cockpit, was powered by a Rolls-Royce Merlin 60 engine, a two-stage, two-speed, inter-cooled powerplant which took development of the Merlin to its ultimate. Like the Mk VI, the VII was a limited production high-altitude interceptor, 140 examples being produced. The aircraft had a service ceiling of 13,420m (44,000ft) and was produced in two variants, the F.VII and HF.VII, the latter with a Merlin 71 engine featuring a Bendix injection carburettor.

Spitfire PR.VII

The Spitfire PR.VII was not a recognized production aircraft, but a service modification of the Mk V; in effect, it was an armed version of the PR.IV, retaining the 'A' type armament of eight Browning 7.7mm (0.303in) machine guns. It had provision for two vertical and one oblique F.24 cameras.

Spitfire Mk VIII (Supermarine Type 359)

The Spitfire Mk VIII was basically an unpressurized version of the Mk VII, intended for low-level air superiority operations. Production reached a total of 1658 aircraft, almost all of which saw service in the Far East and Australia. The major production version was the LF.VIII, with a Merlin 66 engine; the other two variants, the F.VIII and HF.VIII, were respectively fitted with Merlin 61/63 and Merlin 70 engines.

Spitfire Mk IX (Supermarine Type 361)

Early in 1942, the Air Staff envisaged production of both the Spitfire VII and, in much larger numbers, of the Spitfire VIII. The Mk VIII design, however, needed a lot of refinement, including a general strengthening of the fuselage, which meant that production would be delayed for an unacceptably long time, and Air Staff thoughts consequently turned to an interim aircraft: a Mk V Spitfire airframe combined with a Merlin 61 engine. The resulting combination was the Spitfire Mk IX, which for a stop-gap aircraft turned out to be a resounding success. Deliveries to the RAF began in June 1942 and 5665 were built, more than any other mark except the Mk V. The Mk IX was produced in F, LF and HF sub-variants; aircraft with the suffix 'e' (eg LF IXe) featured a universal wing mounting two 20mm cannon outboard and two 12.7mm (0.50in) machine guns inboard.

Spitfire PR.X

The Spitfire PR.X had the shortest operational life of any Spitfire variant, entering service in May 1944 and being discarded in September 1945. Only 16 were built, these being used by No 542 Squadron.

Spitfire PR.XI

The Spitfire PR.XI was a reconnaissance adaptation of the Mk IX; 471 were built, of which 309 were tropicalised for overseas service. Three examples were used by the Royal Navy in the late 1940s, and others were supplied to Greece, the Netherlands, Denmark and Norway.

Spitfire Mk XII (Supermarine Type 366)

The Mk XII, powered by a 1735hp Rolls-Royce Griffon engine, was developed to counter the low-level attacks by German fighter-bombers, mainly the Focke-Wulf Fw 190. It first went into service with No 41 Squadron in February 1943. The squadron shot down its first FW 190 on 27 April, while operating from Hawkinge. The second unit to re-equip with the Mk XII, No 91, destroyed five enemy fighter-bombers in a running battle over the Channel on 25 May 1943. Only 100 MK XII Spitfires were built.

Spitfire PR.XIII

Between December 1942 and May 1943, 18 Spitfire Mk V airframes were fitted with a Rolls-Royce Merlin 32 engine. The type was developed for the low-level tactical reconnaissance role, and remained in service for about two years.

Spitfire Mk XIV (Supermarine Type 379)

Based on a Mk VIII airframe, strengthened to take the extra weight and power of a 2050hp Griffon 65, the Mk XIV was the first Griffon-engined Spitfire variant to go into large-scale production, and the first examples were issued to No 322 (Netherlands) and No 610 Squadrons in March and April 1944. Distinguished from earlier Spitfire marks by its longer nose, cut-down rear fuselage and a clear-view bubble canopy, the Mk XIV was produced in two sub-variants with differing armament fits, as in the Mk.IX. The 527 Mk XIV fighters were complemented by 430 examples of a fighter-reconnaissance version, the FR.XIV, with a fuselage-mounted camera.

Spitfire Mk XVI (Supermarine Type 361)

The Spitfire XVI, which entered service in 1944, was a ground-attack version similar to the Mk IX, but with a Packard-built Merlin 266 engine. It was used in considerable numbers by the RAF at home and abroad in the post-war years, particularly by anti-aircraft co-operation units.

Spitfire F/FR Mk XVIII (Supermarine Type 394)

The Spitfire XVIII was a fighter-reconnaissance variant, just beginning to enter service at the end of WWII, and was the last Griffon-engined development of the original elliptical-wing Spitfire airframe. One hundred were completed as fighters, and a further 200 for the fighter-reconnaissance role. The F/FR XVIII was widely used in the Middle and Far East, and saw action in the early stages of the Malayan Emergency.

Spitfire PR.XIX

The last of the line of photographic reconnaissance Spitfires, and the only PR mark with a Griffon engine, the PR.XIX was basically a late production Mk XIV airframe with a Mk VC bowser wing (a wing adapted for fuel tank stowage) with a universal camera installation based on that of the PR.IV/XI. It was developed early in 1944 to counter German air defences, which were becoming increasingly sophisticated. Production totalled 225 aircraft.

Spitfire Mks 21, 22 and 24

The last variants of the Spitfire, produced until 1947, were the Mks 21, 22 and 24. They bore very little resemblance to the prototype Mk I of a decade earlier. The last of the line, the Mk 24, entered service in November 1946. The Mk 23 was a proposed variant with aerodynamic improvements, which was never built.

Index

Page numbers in *italics* refer to illustrations

Picture Credits

Hugh W. Cowin: 8, 9 (both), 10, 12, 15, 16 (b), 19 (b), 23 (t), 27 (b), 35 (t), 38 (t), 39, 42 (both), 52, 56 (b), 59 (t), 60 (t), 61 (t), 65, 68, 69 (t), 72 (b), 83 (b), 84, 85.

Philip Jarrett: 13, 14, 19 (t), 22, 23 (b), 24 (b), 25, 28, 29 (both), 31, 32, 33 (t), 35 (b), 36 (t), 37, 38 (b), 40, 41, 43, 44 (both), 48, 50–51 (b), 53, 55 (both), 56 (t), 58, 59 (b), 60 (b), 61 (b), 62-63, 66 (b), 67, 69 (b), 70, 71 (t), 74, 75 (both), 76, 77, 78, 79 (both), 80, 81 (both), 82 (both), 83 (t), 86, 87, 88, 89, 90.

TRH: 6, 7, 16 (t) (R. Winslade), 17, 18, 20, 21, 24 (t), 27 (t), 30, 33 (b), 34, 36 (b), 45, 46, 47, 50, 51 (t) (E. Nevill), 54 (both), 57, 64, 66 (b), 71 (b), 72 (t), 73, 91 (R. Winslade), 92 (R. Winslade), 93.

Artworks: Aerospace Publishing